CAMBRIDGE
ENGLISH
Worldwide
Student's Book Three

ANDREW LITTLEJOHN & DIANA HICKS

CAMBRIDGE
UNIVERSITY PRESS

CAMBRIDGE UNIVERSITY PRESS
Cambridge, New York, Melbourne, Madrid, Cape Town, Singapore,
São Paulo, Delhi, Dubai, Tokyo, Mexico City

Cambridge University Press
The Edinburgh Building, Cambridge CB2 8RU, UK

www.cambridge.org
Information on this title: www.cambridge.org/9780521645027

First published 1999
14th printing 2010

Printed in Dubai by Oriental Press

A catalogue record for this publication is available from the British Library

ISBN 978-0-521-64502-7 Student's Book
ISBN 978-0-521-64501-0 Workbook
ISBN 978-0-521-64498-3 Listening and Speaking Pack
ISBN 978-0-521-64500-3 Teacher's Book
ISBN 978-0-521-64499-0 Class Cassette Set
ISBN 978-0-521-77668-4 A to Z of Methodology

Contents

Map of *Cambridge English Worldwide 3*

What's in *Cambridge English Worldwide 3*?

Cambridge English Worldwide 3 has three parts for you, the student. There is a Student's Book, a Workbook and a Listening and Speaking Pack.

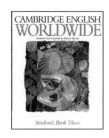
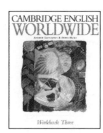

1 A quiz!

1.1 The Student's Book

In which units can you find the pictures?

Look at this book and try to find the answers to these questions.

1 What is the full name of the book?
2 Who published it?
3 Who are the authors?
4 How many units are there? There are six units at the back of the book. How are they different from the others?
5 Where can you find this?
6 What is on page 91? What is it for?

1.2 The Workbook

Look at your Workbook. Write some quiz questions for other students. You can work in teams and have a race!

2 What can you learn about?

Look at the Units in this book. Can you complete this text?

Welcome to *Cambridge English Worldwide 3*

There are six different themes in the book and they are all very interesting! The themes are about a 'Living Museum', mysteries, the environment, _____, _____ and changes in society.

In Themes A–F there are four different types of units: Topic and Language, _____, _____ and Revision. Every theme ends with a page called _____. At the back of the book, there are six _____ _____. If you have time, you can learn about different things in those units. For example, _____, _____, and _____.

While you are learning about a new topic, you can also learn a new language. For example, in Unit _____ you can learn about protecting the environment and also how to talk about the Future in English. In Unit 10, you can learn about _____ and also how to talk about the _____ in English.

The living museum

1 Design a museum

Imagine … They are going to build an exciting new museum and activity centre near you. The museum is going to be about many different things and have LOTS of things to do in it. Here are the names of some of the rooms in the museum.

What other rooms could you have in the museum? What things could you have in each room? Tell the class your ideas.

2 A leaflet

2.1 Things to learn about in the museum

Look at the pictures in the leaflet about the Living Museum. In which room would you put each thing?

2.2 Find the pictures

Look at Units 1–3. Can you find the pictures? What can you learn about in each unit?

AROUND THE THEME

VISIT THE LIVING MUSEUM!

These are some of the many things that you can see, do and learn about in the museum!

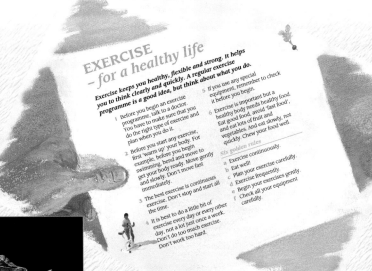

EXERCISE
– for a healthy life

Exercise keeps you healthy, flexible and strong. It helps you to think clearly and quickly. A regular exercise programme is a good idea, but think about what you do.

1 Before you begin an exercise programme, talk to a doctor. You have to make sure that you do the right type of exercise and plan when you do it.

2 Before you start any exercise, first 'warm up' your body. For example, before you begin swimming, bend and move to get your body ready. Move gently and slowly. Don't move fast immediately.

3 The best exercise is continuous exercise. Don't stop and start all the time.

4 It is best to do a little bit of exercise every day or every other day, not a lot just once a week. Don't do too much exercise. Don't work too hard.

5 If you use any special equipment, remember to check it before you begin.

6 Exercise is important but a healthy body needs healthy food. Eat good food, avoid 'fast food', and eat lots of fruit and vegetables. And eat slowly, not quickly. Chew your food well.

Six golden rules

a Exercise continuously.
b Eat well!
c Plan your exercise carefully.
d Exercise frequently.
e Begin your exercises gently.
f Check all your equipment carefully.

The Museum is open every day of the year, from 09.00 to 20.00. Entrance is free of charge. Shop, Restaurant, and Cafe: 09.00 to 19.30.

News about people in your class; getting ready to learn English; Your *Language Record*

1 *Discussion and writing*
WB Ex. 1

2 *Thinking back*

3 *Preparation for learning*

4 *Designing a language record*

1 Moving on

1 Class news

Work in a small group. Tell each other about what you have done recently – last week, in the holidays, at the weekend.

> Last week, I went to the mountains with my family.

> In the holidays, I got a new bicycle. It's a mountain bike.

> Last weekend, I played the guitar in a concert.

> We went walking for two days.

Now, write something about yourself for a 'Class news' poster. Ask the people in your group to help you with ideas, spelling, grammar and vocabulary. Later, you can add some photographs and pictures.

2 The English you learned

Work by yourself. Think for a few moments. What did you learn from your last English book? What topics did you study?

3 A new beginning

You can help yourself in class if you ask questions and if you tell the teacher when you need help. Work with your neighbour. What can you say in English in these situations? Make a list.

A classroom phrasebook

a You don't know how to write a word.
b You can't hear the cassette.
c You weren't in the class last lesson.
d You can't pronounce a word in English.
e You don't know what a word means.
f You don't know how to translate a word from your language.
g Your teacher is speaking too fast.
h You didn't hear what the teacher said.
i You want to use a dictionary.
j You haven't got a pen with you.
k You don't understand.
l You have finished your work.

What grammar did you learn?
What vocabulary areas can you remember?
What activities did you do? Make some notes about what you can remember.

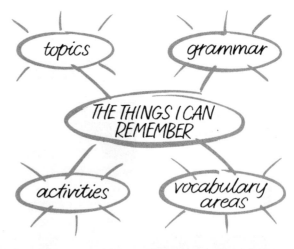

Compare your ideas with your neighbour.

What did you enjoy doing? What did you find difficult? What would you like to do again? Tell the class what you think.

4 Your Language Record

4.1 Look at the Units

In Book 3, many exercises tell you what are the important things to learn and make notes about. For example, find these exercises in Theme B. What are they about?

Unit 4, Exercise 6

Unit 5, Exercise 7

Look at Theme C. Can you find similar exercises in Units 7 and 8?

4.2 Prepare your *Language Record*

Get a large exercise book.
Divide it into three sections.

Use your *Language Record* book to note down the language you learn in Book 3.

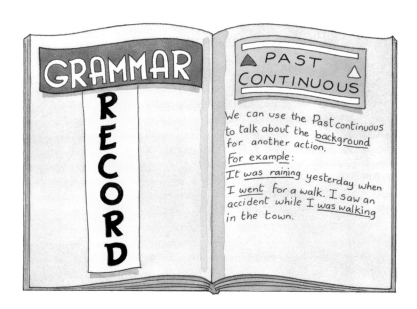

A test covering social language, special verbs, adverbs, Past simple, Past continuous

1 *Special verbs' and adverbs*
WB Ex. 1
2 *Past simple*
3 *Past simple, irregular verbs, questions*
4 *Past continuous*

2 The living museum
Test your English

Find out how much English you know and discover what's in the different rooms in the museum!

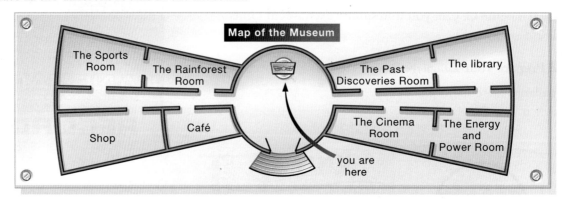

Map of the Museum

The Sports Room
The Rainforest Room
The Past Discoveries Room
The library
Shop
Café
The Cinema Room
The Energy and Power Room
you are here

1 In the sports room

1.1 The decathlon

In a decathlon, you have to do ten different sports.

do the pole vault

throw the javelin

jump over hurdles

throw the shot

Steve Johnson is a decathlete. He enjoys some sports more than others.

HATES	DOESN'T MIND
discus	100 metres
shot	hurdles
	javelin
LIKES	LOVES
400 metres	1,500 metres
high jump	long jump
pole vault	

Write three sentences about him.
For example:

He likes doing the pole vault.

1.2 How does Steve do it?

Circle the correct word.

1 For all the decathlon events Steve trains ....
   a hardly   b hard   c softly
2 He jumps the hurdles ....
   a good   b well   c high
3 He throws the javelin ....
   a careful   b long   c carefully

2 In the rainforest room

Read about the okapi. Write the correct past form of the verb for each gap.

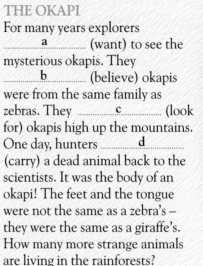

THE OKAPI
For many years explorers ....a........... (want) to see the mysterious okapis. They ....b........... (believe) okapis were from the same family as zebras. They ....c........... (look for) okapis high up the mountains. One day, hunters ....d........... (carry) a dead animal back to the scientists. It was the body of an okapi! The feet and the tongue were not the same as a zebra's – they were the same as a giraffe's. How many more strange animals are living in the rainforests?

3 In the past discoveries room: China

3.1 Jing Di: 157–141BC

Circle the correct answer.

An important discovery

1 In 1990, builders .... working on a road
   to the new airport at Xian, China.
   a is beginning   b began   c begin

2 The builders .... that in some places the
   earth was not flat.
   a see   b sees   c saw

3 They .... archaeologists to check the site.
   a told   b tell   c are telling

4 When archaeologists .... to the
   site they discovered that it was full of different things.
   It was the burial site of Emperor Jing Di.
   a go   b went   c goes

3.2 In the burial site

Read about the burial sites.

Jing Di's burial site

Hundreds of artists, craftsmen and builders worked for
many years to prepare the things for the burial places. For
example, in one burial place, there were small models of
different animals – dogs, sheep and cows. In another burial
place, they found 70 soldiers about 60 cm high. These
model soldiers all had different faces – some were sad,
some were happy , some were thoughtful. They also found
an enormous quantity of cereal. The emperor wanted to
take food with him to eat on his journey to another world.

Write three questions about the text.

How many <u>soldiers did they find</u> ?

1 What .... ?

2 Where .... ?

3 Why .... ?

3.3 Right or wrong?

Read the text in Exercise 3.2 again. Correct
the information in these sentences. For
example:

Jing Di came from Japan.

No, he didn't come from Japan.
He came from China.

1 Real soldiers went with Jing Di into his burial
   place. *No, ...*
2 All the soldiers had the same faces. *No, ...*
3 Jing Di took real animals into his burial
   place. *No, ...*

4 In the energy and power room

Read the dialogue. Choose the correct answer.

GUIDE: Come on everyone. It's 6 o'clock.
        You .... go home now.

MARK: Oh no! Is it really 6 o'clock?

STEPHANIE: Aren't you going to see all the
            different batteries?

MARK: No, I .... to finish my
       experiment.
       2 a go   2 b going to
       2 c am going to

STEPHANIE: An experiment? What are
            you .... do?
            3 a were you doing   3 b going to
            3 c go to

MARK: Well, I'm going to put a piece of
       copper wire into one side of the
       lemon and the xinc wire into the
       other side ...

STEPHANIE: Yes. And then what do you
            ....
            4 a have to do 4 b having to
            4 c doing

MARK: I don't know! I have to read the
       instructions.

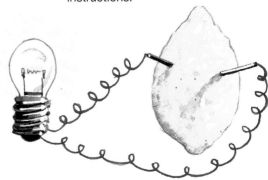

Revision
exercises after
the Unit 2 test
WB Unit 3: Extra
practice

1 *Adverbs,
'special verbs'*

2 *Simple past,
regular verbs*
WB EX. 1

3 Around the museum again

1 In the sports room

1.1 Exercise for a healthy life

Can you match each paragraph 1–6 with a 'golden rule' a–f?

Adverbs are words that describe *how* you do something. Read the leaflet again and make a list of the adverbs (e.g. *gently*). There are 11 different adverbs. Can you find three that don't have *-ly* on the end?

EXERCISE
– for a healthy life

Exercise keeps you healthy, flexible and strong. It helps you to think clearly and quickly. A regular exercise programme is a good idea, but think about what you do.

1 Before you begin an exercise programme, talk to a doctor. You have to make sure that you do the right type of exercise and plan when you do it.

2 Before you start any exercise, first 'warm up' your body. For example, before you begin swimming, bend and move to get your body ready. Move gently and slowly. Don't move fast immediately.

3 The best exercise is continuous exercise. Don't stop and start all the time.

4 It is best to do a little bit of exercise every day or every other day, not a lot just once a week. Don't do too much exercise. Don't work too hard.

5 If you use any special equipment, remember to check it before you begin.

6 Exercise is important but a healthy body needs healthy food. Eat good food, avoid 'fast food', and eat lots of fruit and vegetables. And eat slowly, not quickly. Chew your food well.

Six golden rules

a Exercise continuously.
b Eat well!
c Plan your exercise carefully.
d Exercise frequently.
e Begin your exercises gently.
f Check all your equipment carefully.

1.2 An interview with Steve Johnson

Read an interview with Steve Johnson.
What does Steve like doing?
What does he hate doing?

Interview with Steve Johnson, decathlete

INTERVIEWER:	Steve, why did you become a decathlete?
STEVE:	Well, I loved running at school and doing long jumps. When I left school, I got a job in an office but I hated working inside. I didn't like sitting down all day.
INTERVIEWER:	So what did you do?
STEVE:	I left the office job and I started working in a sports centre. I enjoyed helping people with their exercise programmes.
INTERVIEWER:	But in a sports centre you're inside most of the day, aren't you?
STEVE:	Well, I don't mind being inside if I can move!
INTERVIEWER:	Are you training a lot now, Steve?
STEVE:	Oh, yes. I began training a lot about a year ago. I want to be in the next Olympics, you know!
INTERVIEWER:	And do you like training?
STEVE:	Oh, yes, I enjoy it very much.
INTERVIEWER:	Well, good luck with the Olympics, Steve!
STEVE:	Thanks!

Some verbs in English are 'special'. The verb *after* them usually has '–ing' at the end. For example:

I loved running at school.

Can you find six more special verbs in the interview?

Use the verbs to write about the sports that you like.

2 In the rainforest room

India
The Philippines
Thailand
Indonesia

2.1 The mystery of the Tasaday people

Read a true story about the Tasaday people in the Philippines.
Can you complete the story with the correct form of the verbs?

An important discovery – the Tasaday people

In 1971, in the Philippines, some men 1.................. (discover) a group of 25 people in the rainforest. They were called the Tasaday people and they 2.................. (live) like cave people from thousands of years ago. They had fire but they did not use the wheel. This was important world news – they were stone age people in the 20th century!

Many scientists 3.................. (want) to learn more about them so they 4.................. (ask) them lots of questions. They also 5.................. (live) with them for a long time. The Tasadays did not have agriculture – they 6..................

(collect) plants to eat and 7.................. (trap) fish in the river. They were very peaceful people. They 8.................. (believe) that the animals were their natural friends.

The scientists 9.................. (stay) with the Tasadays for a long time but then a war 10.................. (start) in the Philippines and they 11.................. (return) to the cities. Many countries gave money to the Philippines government to make sure the Tasaday people were safe. The government 12.................. (stop) all tree-cutting and road building in the area.

2.2 What didn't they have?

The Tasadays lived like cave people. What things didn't they have, do you think? Write five or six sentences and then compare with your neighbour. For example:

They didn't have cars.

2.3 The Tasadays – was it a trick?

Read more about the Tasaday story.
Was it a trick? Tell the class what you think.

Was it a trick?

A few months later, a journalist visited the Tasadays. When he arrived he discovered that the Tasadays lived in houses not caves. They watched television and they had modern clothes. He asked them what happened.

'A big company wanted to build a road here', they said. 'A man called Elizande wanted to save the forest. He gave us money and asked us to live like cave people.'

The journalist took photographs of the Tasadays in their houses and wrote about it in the newspapers – 'The Tasaday Trick' it said. The scientists were very angry and they went back to see the Tasadays. When they arrived, they saw that the Tasadays lived in caves, not houses. They did not have television or electricity. They were stone age cave people.

Were the Tasadays stone age people? Perhaps the journalist wanted to write a good story. Perhaps *he* gave them money and asked them to live in houses. Or perhaps the scientists wanted to save the forest. What do you think?

3 **In the past discoveries room: the Mayan civilisation**

3.1 The Maya route

Read about the Mayas and complete the text with the correct form of each verb. (The list of irregular verbs on page 90 can help you.)

Palenque, Mexico

The Mayan Civilisation

The Mayan civilisation 1.............................. (begin) more than 3,000 years ago and 2.............................. (become) powerful and rich. The Mayas 3.............................. (understand) astronomy and could predict eclipses of the sun and moon. They 4.............................. (write) in pictures and 5.............................. (do) complex mathematical calculations. They also travelled to other countries and 6.............................. (buy) and 7.............................. (sell) things.

Mayan designs

For hundreds of years, the forests 8.............................. (hide) many enormous Mayan cities and pyramids, such as Palenque, Mexico. The cities of Tikal and El Mirador, in Guatemala, for example, probably 9.............................. (have) populations of more than 55,000 before the people mysteriously 10.............................. (leave) in 900 AD.

Mayan stonework

Ten years ago the governments of Mexico, Belize, Guatemala, Honduras and El Salvador 11.............................. (come) together and 12.............................. (make) 'La Ruta Maya', a 2,300-kilometre road around the Mayan land to help historians discover more about the fantastic Mayan culture. Today, there are more than four million Mayas and they live in the same area as the great Mayan civilisation.

3.2 Where is it?

Write the past form of the verbs from Exercise 3.1 in the puzzle. Find the name of a country.

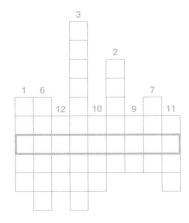

3.3 The Mayan past: Copan, Honduras

Ricardo Fasquelle is an archaeologist. He works at the ancient Mayan city of Copan. Read his answers and write the questions.

YOU:	When ....?
MR FASQUELLE:	We started work here in 1978.
YOU:	What ....?
MR FASQUELLE:	We wanted to find out more about the lives of the ordinary Mayan people.
YOU:	What ....?
MR FASQUELLE:	They ate corn, beans, rabbit, deer and a vegetable called 'squash'.
YOU:	Why ....?
MR FASQUELLE:	They came because the land was very good.

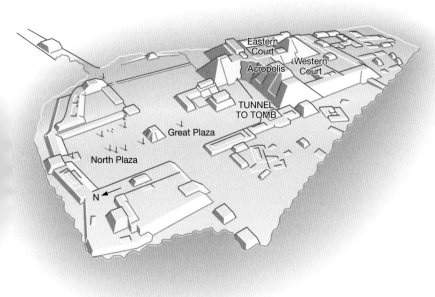

YOU:	When ....?
MR FASQUELLE:	About 3,000 years ago.
YOU:	When ....?
MR FASQUELLE:	We think they left about 950 AD.
YOU:	Why ....?
MR FASQUELLE:	They probably left because there was not enough water for all the people.
YOU:	How ....?
MR FASQUELLE:	Well, we got a lot of information when we dug into the tombs.
YOU:	That's very interesting. Thank you, Mr Fasquelle.

3.4 True or false

Read Exercises 3.1 and 3.3 again. Are these sentences true or false? Correct them if they are wrong.

1 The Mayas left their cities because of wars.

   False! The Mayas didn't leave because of wars.
   They left because there wasn't enough water.

2 The Mayas wrote in Spanish.

3 The Mayas came from Europe.

4 The Mayas only ate vegetables.

5 The Mayas all died in 950 AD.

6 The Mayas had big towns and cities.

Work by yourself. Answer the questions in the questionnaire.

Discuss your answers with other students in your class. How can you make your groupwork better?

Questionnaire
Groupwork

What happens when you work in a group?
Tick (✓) the sentences that are true for you.

- [ ] **1** We usually work very well together.
- [ ] **2** It is difficult for us to work together.
- [ ] **3** We don't like working in groups.

Planning

- [ ] **4** We often don't agree what we are going to do.
- [ ] **5** We usually agree *who* is going to do different parts of the task.
- [ ] **6** We usually agree *how long* we are going to spend on different parts of the task.

Working together

- [ ] **7** Everybody in the group does the same amount of work.
- [ ] **8** One or two people don't do anything.
- [ ] **9** One or two people do most of the work.

Time

- [ ] **10** We usually don't finish.
- [ ] **11** We spend too much time talking and not enough time writing.
- [ ] **12** We spend a lot of time talking before we start working.

By yourself, look at Units 1–3 and find an exercise where you worked in a group. Write down some good points and bad points about your groupwork. Then, discuss your points with students you worked with. How can you work together differently next time?

Theme B

A world of mystery

1 What do you think?

Do you believe in ghosts?
Do you believe in magic?
Is there a logical explanation for everything?

Do you know any mysteries? Tell the class your ideas.

2 Take a look at Theme B

2.1 Great mysteries

Look at the pictures on the cover of the book. What mystery do you think each picture is about?

2.2 Find the pictures

Look at Units 4–6 and Optional Unit B. Where can you find the pictures? What are they about? Check your answers to Exercise 2.1.

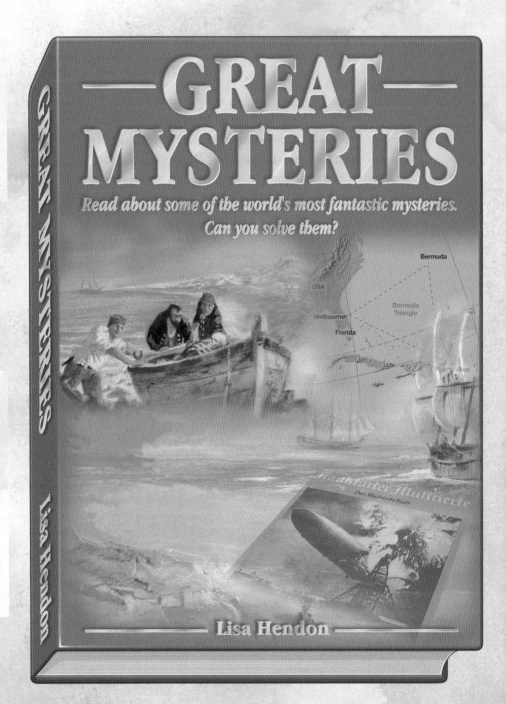

GREAT MYSTERIES

Read about some of the world's most fantastic mysteries. Can you solve them?

Lisa Hendon

The mystery of
Franklin's Arctic
expedition;
modals;
'anybody/thing';
Past continuous;
curriculum links
with History and
Geography

1 *Discussion*
2 *Reading*
IT A and B

Inside the text
A *Comprehension*
B *'anybody/
    any …'*

WB Ex. 3

4 The Franklin mystery
Topic and language

1 On top of the world

1.1 What's it like?

Look at the map and the picture of the Arctic.
Is it a nice place? Why/Why not?
Who lives there, do you think? What do they
eat? Where do they live? What animals and
plants live there?
Tell the class your ideas.

1.2 A trip to the Arctic

Imagine you are going to make a trip by ship
from Europe to Alaska. Work with a partner
and look at the map. Make some notes about
these things.

A possible route
The things we should take
Possible problems

Tell the class your ideas.

We can go from … to …
We should take lots of food. We should take …
We might hit an iceberg. We might …

2 The Franklin Expedition

2.1 England, 1845

In 1845, John Franklin left England with 134
men. He wanted to find a way to the
northwest of Canada.
Look at the list of supplies on Franklin's ships.
Which things are the most important, do you
think? Why?
Look at the 'Reward' notice. What happened
to Franklin, do you think?

2.2 What happened to them?

Work with your neighbour. Read about the
Franklin mystery. Write the correct paragraph
number for each sentence.

Paragraph ☐ says what the British government did.
Paragraph ☐ says why Franklin went to the Arctic.
Paragraph ☐ says what some sailors found.
Paragraph ☐ says what Franklin took with him.
Paragraph ☐ says who saw Franklin for the last
time.

Look at the list of supplies on Franklin's ships,
the 'Reward' notice and the graves. Can you
find a mistake in the information in the text?

🔊 The story is also on the cassette.

The mystery of the Franklin Expedition

Many years ago, explorers wanted to find a way by sea from Europe to China, via Alaska. In 1845, John Franklin left England with 134 men to look for a route through the Arctic.

Franklin's ships had everything they needed. They had enough food in tins for three years and thousands of litres of lemon juice to stop disease. They also had two libraries with 3,000 books, excellent maps, scientific instruments, musical instruments and a new invention: a camera.

Franklin and his men left England on May 19th, 1845 and they sailed without problems across the Atlantic towards Canada. When Franklin arrived at Baffin Bay in July 1845, things were going very well for the expedition. On July 26th, some sailors saw Franklin's ships when they were entering the bay. That was the last time that anyone saw Franklin and his men alive.

Supplies on Franklin's Ships

8,000 tins of meat, soup and vegetables
900 litres of wine for the sick
4,250 kilograms of chocolate
1,000 kilograms of tea
62,000 kilograms of flour
17,000 litres of rum
3,200 kilograms of tobacco
4,200 litres of lemon juice

Toronto Globe 4 April 1850

The Franklin Expedition
REWARD
£20,000

For any person who can help the Franklin Expedition

The British government became very worried when they heard nothing from Franklin. They sent expeditions to look for him, but the expeditions all returned without any news. The government offered £20,000 to anybody who could help Franklin or anybody who had information about Franklin. Nobody came with information.

Then, in August 1850 some sailors found the first signs of the Franklin Expedition while they were searching on Devon Island: some old food tins, some papers, and, something very strange, the graves of three men. The men all died in January 1846 while Franklin was waiting in Baffin Bay for the ice to melt. But why did they die? The three men were all young and three deaths in the first months of the expedition was very strange. What happened to them? And where were the ships and all the other sailors? The mystery of the Franklin Expedition was growing stronger …

WILLIAM BRAINE
DIED APRIL 3rd 1846
AGED 32 YEARS

JOHN HARTNELL
DIED JANUARY 4th 1846
AGED 25 YEARS

JOHN TORRINGTON
DIED JANUARY 1st 1846
AGED 20 YEARS

Inside the text

A Notes about the expedition

Can you complete these notes about the Franklin Expedition?

> The Franklin Expedition
> Franklin left England in 1845.
> _ _ _ _ _ _ _ _ _ _ _ _ _ _ three years.
> _ _ _ _ _ _ _ _ _ _ _ _ Baffin Bay.
> _ _ _ _ _ _ _ _ _ _ _ _ _ _ £20,000.
> In 1850, some sailors found _ _ _ _ _ _
> This was very strange because _ _ _ _
> _

B Anybody can do it

In Books 1 and 2, you saw how you can use 'any' in negative sentences, like this:

> There wasn't any sign of Franklin's ships.

You can also use 'any' in positive sentences to mean 'not a particular person/thing/place'.

> Some sailors saw Franklin in July 1946. That was the last time anyone saw Franklin.

Choose the correct word or words to complete each sentence.

anybody   anywhere   any time   any games
any book   anywhere

1 .... can learn to speak a foreign language.
2 This plant can grow ....
3 Tomorrow I'm having a party at home. You can come to my house at .... Bring .... that you have.
4 In the library you can borrow .... that you like.
5 Come in! Sit down. You can sit .... you want.

3 At sea

3.1 Sounds from the sea

📼 Listen to some sounds from the sea. What can you hear?

3.2 Imagine …

You are a sailor on Franklin's ship. It is July 1845 and you are in Baffin Bay. Note down your answers to these questions.

What are you doing now?
How do you feel? How is the food?
What is happening on the ship?
Are things going well or badly? Why?
What do you do when you aren't on duty?

Now, using your notes, write part of a diary.

We left England two months ago.
The journey is going very well/badly.
The ship is…
At this moment I am…
When I am not on duty I…
The food…
We eat…

4 Language focus Past continuous

4.1 In your language

How do you say these sentences in your language?

When Franklin arrived at Baffin Bay in July 1845, things were going very well.
Some sailors saw Franklin's ships when they were entering the bay.

Underline the verbs in each sentence. What do you notice about the form of the verbs? How are they different? Can you find some more examples in the text in Exercise 2.2?

4.2 What's it for?

In Books 1 and 2, you saw four main verb forms:

The *Present simple* for descriptions or habits:

Jack lives in a big house.

The *Past simple* for actions that are finished:

Cave people lived thousands of years ago.

The *Present continuous* for actions that are happening now:

Look! It's raining!

or for future plans:

I'm working tomorrow.

'*going to*' to talk about the future:

I'm going to visit my uncle next week.

Another verb form is the *Past continuous*.

They found the graves while **they were searching** on Devon Island.

When do you think you use it? Look at these examples and tell the class your ideas.

The men died while Franklin was waiting in Baffin Bay.
It was raining yesterday when I went for a walk.
I saw an accident while I was walking in the town.

Which actions are the background for other actions? What verb form do you use after 'while'? You can also say 'when' instead of 'while'.

They found the graves when they were searching on Devon Island.

4.3 What were you doing?

Work with a partner. Ask each other questions. Invent some details. like this:

A: *I broke my brother's computer last night.*
B: *How? What were you doing?*
A: *I was sitting on it!*
B: *What did you do about it?*
A: *I told him. He wasn't very happy.*

Some ideas:

I swallowed a bee yesterday.
Heidi lost her watch last night.
Peter fell off a ladder last week.
I saw a mouse last night.
Omar and Esta found £10 this morning.

The last message

In England, many people wanted to know more about Franklin. Some people said that Franklin and his men were living with the Eskimo people or 'Inuit'. Other people said that Franklin was certainly dead.

Jane Franklin was John Franklin's wife. She wanted to know exactly what happened to her husband. In July 1857, she sent an expedition to the Arctic. A year later, on an island in Baffin Bay, they discovered one of Franklin's sailors – ten years too late. He was lying in a boat at the edge of the sea – dead.

Near the dead man, they found a small stone house. Inside the house they found a note. It was the last message from the Franklin Expedition.

So, Franklin and his men died in the Arctic – three years after they left England. Without any food, their only chance was to walk to their deaths in the ice. The Franklin mystery was solved.

But was it solved? Why were so many sailors dying when they left the ships? Franklin had excellent maps of the area. Why did he take the wrong route? There were still questions to answer …

April 25th 1848
We arrived here in September 1846 – nineteen months ago. Our ships are trapped in the ice and we cannot move. The men are dying – 25 men are already dead. Captain John Franklin died on June 11th 1847. We left the ships two days ago. Our only chance now is to walk.

5 The mystery of the Franklin Expedition, Part 2

 Read (and listen to) the next part of the Franklin mystery.

Why do you think so many men were dying when they left the ships? Why did Franklin take the wrong route, do you think?

6 Your Language Record

6.1 Your Grammar Record

Make notes about the Past continuous in your *Grammar Record*. Make notes about how to form it and how to use it. Look at Exercise 4 and the Language summaries in your Workbook for ideas.

6.2 Your Record of Language Use

Look at Unit 4. Are there more words and phrases you can add to your *Record of Language Use*? Check your record with this list.

Verbs explore sail search melt cross (the Atlantic) might should agree divide belong fail step onto

Nouns explorer exploration route disease government reward sign grave death Inuit edge note message chance

Adjectives enough worried strange undisturbed

Time to spare?

Choose one of these exercises.

1 Look at the *Help yourself list* on page 91. Make an exercise about this Unit.

2 Complete the gaps with the correct form of the verb.

Last night I _was sleeping_ (sleep) in my cabin, when I .... (hear) a terrible noise. I .... (get up) immediately and .... (run) outside. The wind .... (blow) very hard and it .... (rain) very heavily. The waves .... (splash) over the side of the ship. Jack Smith .... (tie) a rope when a big wave .... (hit) him. He .... (fall) on the floor and .... (break) his leg. It was a very bad storm. It lasted for over two hours.

3 Write a conversation between Jane Franklin and the leader of the 1857 expedition, after they have returned to England. Act it out for the class.

Mysteries;
expressing cause
and effect; modal
verbs; curriculum
links with Science,
History and Moral
Education

5 Mysteries solved?
Topic and language

1 Mysteries that you know

Are there any famous mysteries in your
country?
Do you know any mysteries from other
countries?
Tell the class your ideas.

2 Some more mysteries

2.1 Mysteries from the world of travel

Read about each mystery. Find the answers to
these questions.

Which stories are from the United States?
Which stories are about mysteries at sea?
Which stories are about mysteries in the air?
Which story is the most mysterious, do you
think? Why?

2.2 What do you think?

Work with your neighbour. Read about the
Bermuda Triangle, the *Marie Celeste* and the
Hindenburg again. Can you explain what
happened? Make some notes about your ideas
and tell the class. For example:

The Bermuda Triangle
Perhaps the weather is very bad in the
area.
Perhaps ...

3 Mystery solved?

3.1 What are they talking about?

[cassette] Listen to part of a radio programme.
Mike Brown is talking to Lisa Hendon, the
author of a book about famous mysteries.

Which mysteries are they talking about?
Does Lisa Hendon think that mysteries really
exist?

3.2 Listen again, listen carefully

[cassette] Listen to each part of the conversation
once or twice again. What is Lisa Hendon's
explanation for each mystery?

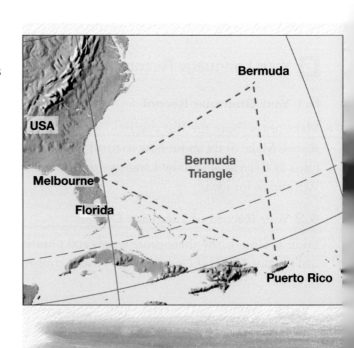

4 Language focus Cause and effect

Notice how you can describe something that usually happens. What tense do you use in each part of the sentence?

> When things move, they sometimes collect static electricity.
> When water reaches 0°C, it freezes.

You can also say what always happens if you do something.

> If you throw something up, it comes down.
> If you don't eat, you get ill.

Work with a partner. Can you complete these sentences?

When water reaches 100°C, …   **When the sun goes down, …**   **When winter comes, …**

If you don't go to school, …   **If you touch something very hot, …**   **If you drink petrol, …**

Write the beginnings of some more 'When …' and 'If …' sentences. Give them to another pair of students to complete.

Mystery in the air

The *Hindenburg* was an airship that flew from Germany to America. In 1936, it made over ten successful trips but then in 1937, a terrible accident happened.

When it was arriving in the United States, it suddenly exploded into flames. Thirty-six people died in the accident. Why did it explode? Where did the flames come from? It is still a complete mystery why the accident happened.

The mystery of the Bermuda Triangle

The Bermuda Triangle is an area in the Atlantic Ocean, near Florida in the United States. Some years ago, many aeroplanes disappeared when they were flying through the area. Ships also disappeared or sank when they were sailing there. Today, many people say that the area has a special, magical force and that it is very dangerous. They are frightened of going into the area because they say something might happen to them.

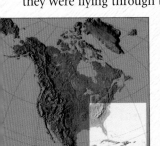

Mystery at sea

One of the greatest sea mysteries of all time is the *Marie Celeste*. The *Marie Celeste* was a large ship that sailed from New York in 1872. Two months later, sailors in another ship met The *Marie Celeste* in the Atlantic. They came near the ship to speak to the captain, but they discovered there was absolutely nobody on the ship. Everything else on the ship was completely normal. There weren't any signs of a fight, or illness or any other problems. Where did everyone go?

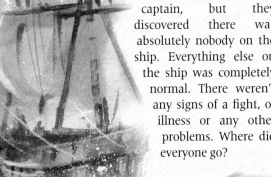

5 **Language focus** '**should, might, need, must**'

5.1 In your language

How do you say these sentences in your language?

I should see Peter tomorrow.
I must see Peter tomorrow.
I might see Peter tomorrow.
I need to see Peter tomorrow.

'Should', 'might', 'need' and 'must' are called 'modal verbs'. Look at the sentences again. What form of the verb comes after 'should', 'might', and 'must'? What form of the verb comes after 'need'?

5.2 What should they do?

Work with your neighbour. Look at this list of people. What should they do? What should they be able to do? Write down your ideas about some of them. Compare ideas with other students.

teachers   children   mothers   fathers
police officers   doctors

For example, do you agree with these sentences?

Children should do four hours' homework every night.
Children should do all the cooking and cleaning at home.
Children should go to bed at 6.00.
Children should be able to smoke.

5.3 You mustn't do that!

Be careful! The negative of 'must' isn't 'mustn't'! Look:

I must do my Maths homework tonight.
I <u>don't have to</u> do my English homework.

'mustn't' means 'it is not allowed':

You mustn't drop rubbish in the street.

Look at the pictures of different places. What mustn't you do there? Write about some of them. Compare ideas with other students.

in the street

on a bus or train

in a cinema

in a classroom

6 **The mystery of the Franklin Expedition, the final part**

In 1984, a scientist solved the Franklin mystery. Look at the pictures and think. Why do you think so many sailors died? How do you think the scientist found out?

🔲 Read (and listen to) the final part of the Franklin mystery and check your answers.

Mystery solved?

1984, One hundred and forty years later

Dr Owen Beattie was a scientist at a university in Canada. He wanted to know why so many men died in the Franklin Expedition.

Dr Beattie began to think about the first men who died on the expedition. They were all young and they died after only six months at sea. Twenty more men died the next year. There was something very strange about this and there was only one way to discover what it was.

In 1984, Dr Beattie went to Baffin Bay with a team of scientists. There, they opened the graves of the three Franklin sailors. Because of the extreme cold and ice, the bodies were in perfect condition. Beattie took small samples of hair and skin and then put the bodies back into the graves.

Back at the university, Beattie made an incredible discovery. From the hair and skin, he found that the three men died from lead poisoning. They had nearly *100 times* more lead in their bodies than normal.

Lead was inside Franklin's food tins.

But where did the lead come from? Beattie looked closely at some of Franklin's food tins and found the answer. In those days, tins were closed with lead. Usually, this was not a big problem, but these tins were not made correctly. Lead was *inside* the tins. It was not the ice and cold that killed the men. It was the 8,000 tins of food that they were eating.

Lead also affects the brain. It makes it difficult to think clearly. Up in the Arctic, we can now understand why John Franklin made so many wrong decisions.

7 Your Language Record

7.1 Your Grammar Record

Make notes about describing cause and effect in your *Grammar Record*. Make notes about how to form sentences with modals and what they mean. Look at Exercises 5 and 6 and the Language summaries in your Workbook for ideas.

7.2 Your Record of Language Use

Look back at Unit 5. Are there more words and phrases you can add to your *Record of Language Use*? Check your record with this list.

Nouns area condition explanation flame force hydrogen illness lead mystery poisoning sample spark static electricity theory tin

Verbs affect disappear explode sink (sank, sunk)

Adverbs absolutely carefully clearly closely completely correctly

Time to spare?

Choose one of these exercises.

1 Look at the *Help yourself list* on page 91. Make an exercise about this Unit.

2 Think about next week. Make some notes under these headings.

   Next week,
   I should ...   I must ...   I might ...
   I need to ...   I mustn't ...

3 What should the following people do in their jobs? Write about each one.

   dentists actors chefs architects football players musicians

FOCUS ON
Exploration

1 The world of exploration

1.1 Search!

Look at the pictures and the texts on page 27. Can you find answers to these questions?

1 Why are there pyramids in Latin America, according to Thor Heyerdahl?
2 Who used a 'land bridge'? Where did they go?
3 Why do people speak Portuguese in Brazil today?

Write some more 'search' questions for other students.

1.2 When did it happen?

Read through each text and make a note of the dates. Can you put the information in chronological order? For example:

40,000 years ago: People arrived in America.
10,000 years ago:

2 Decide ...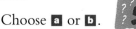

Choose a or b.

a How did it change our world?

Look at the texts and pictures again. What happened as a result of each event? Use your imagination and general knowledge and write a result for each event b–e.

Events

a People crossed into America from Asia.
b People perhaps travelled from Egypt to America.
c Spain and Portugal divided the world in half.
d Magellan went around the world.

For example:

Results
a There are Native Americans ('Indians') in America now.

Can you think of more explorations and their result today?

b You decide!

Decide what *you* want to do and ask your teacher. You could:

– write a newspaper story from 1642.
– write a diary for a day on Thor Heyerdahl's boat.
– write a poem about the Arctic.
– write about some other explorations.
– write a conversation between Magellan and the King.

Look at the *Help yourself list* on page 91 for ideas.

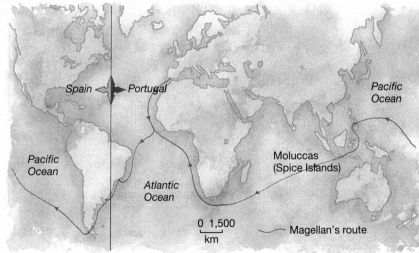

Heyerdahl's boat, Ra II

Pyramids in Egypt and in America – why and how?

Did people travel from Egypt to America 4,000 years ago? Thor Heyerdahl, a Norwegian explorer, thinks so. To test his idea, Heyerdahl made a simple boat, similar to the ancient Egyptian boats. Then, in May 1970, with eight men on his boat, he sailed from Africa. Two months later, in July 1970, he arrived in Barbados. Heyerdahl showed that it was possible for the ancient Egyptians to cross the Atlantic. He thinks that this might explain why there are pyramids in Egypt and Latin America.

40,000 years ago

The first people in America

The first people in America probably arrived there about 40,000 years ago, during the ice age. Because of the ice, the sea level was lower than it is today and there was dry land between Asia and North America. People crossed over the land and travelled south into North and South America. Later, about 10,000 years ago, the climate changed and the ice melted. The level of the sea rose and the 'land bridge' disappeared.

Pyramids in Egypt

Pyramids in Mexico

The first journey around the world

Most explorations were for two reasons: power and money. In 1494, Spain and Portugal agreed to divide the non-Christian world between them. They drew a line on a map and said that everything to the west belonged to Spain, everything to the east belonged to Portugal. (For this reason, people in Brazil speak Portuguese today.)

The King of Spain wanted the Moluccas (or 'Spice Islands') so, in 1519, he sent Ferdinand Magellan to prove that they were in the west. Magellan found a way around South America into an enormous ocean. He called the ocean the 'Pacific'. Magellan was murdered in the Phillipines in 1521, but his ships continued back to Spain and arrived there in 1522. They became the first ships to go all around the world.

Today

Work by yourself. Answer the questions in the questionnaire. Discuss your answers with other students in your class. How can you do your homework better?

Questionnaire
Homework

1 Do you do your homework?
- ❏ always
- ❏ usually
- ❏ sometimes
- ❏ almost never

Why?

2 Where do you usually do your homework?
- ❏ in a quiet place
- ❏ in a noisy place
- ❏ at a table
- ❏ lying on my bed
- ❏ while I am watching TV
- ❏ while I am eating
- ❏ Some other place:

3 If you know that you won't have time to do all your homework, what do you do?
- ❏ I don't do it.
- ❏ I try to do some of it.
- ❏ I try to do it earlier, when I have time.
- ❏ I cancel my other activities (sports, games, etc.).
- ❏ I explain to the teacher that I won't have time.
- ❏ Something else:

4 What do you do if you haven't done your homework?
- ❏ I don't go to school.
- ❏ I copy from a friend.
- ❏ I explain to the teacher why I haven't done it.
- ❏ I go to school and hope the teacher won't check.
- ❏ I ask my parents to write a note.
- ❏ Something else:

5 Do you think homework is useful? Why/why not?

6 Do you think you get too much homework? How much is a 'good' amount?

By yourself, look back at Units 2–6 and find some exercises which you did for homework. Try to find some homework you did well and some you did not so well. Write down as many reasons as you can why you think you did some pieces of work better than the others. Compare your ideas with others in your class.

1 Our present, our future

Look at the cover of the *Green Earth* magazine.
Note down your answers to these questions.

Which pictures show positive images of the environment? Why?
Which pictures show negative images of the environment? Why?
Which pictures are about nature?
Which pictures are about life in towns?

Tell the class your ideas.

AROUND THE THEME

2 Take a look at Theme C

2.1 In this issue

Look at the magazine cover again.
Read 'In this issue'. Can you match
each section to one of the small pictures
at the side of the magazine cover?

2.2 Find the pictures.

Look at Units 7–9.
Where can you find the pictures?
Check your answers to Exercise 2.1.

Green Earth

Issue number 53   Spring

FOCUS ON OUR ENVIRONMENT
SAVE THE EARTH!

IN THIS ISSUE
- *Problems for the environment*
- *Alternative transport*
- *How YOU can help the Earth*
- *Life in the future?*

Ecology;
curriculum links
with Environmental
Science; Present
perfect

1 *Discussion*
2 *Reading*
WB Ex. 1, IT A
and B

Inside the text
A *Comprehension*
B *Comprehension*
WB Ex. 2

7 Our environment
Topic and language

1 Our changing environment

1.1 The environment today

Discuss these questions with your class.

How is the environment changing?
What problems are there in the environment today, do you think?
Are there environmental problems where you live?
What are people doing to help the environment?

1.2 What is it?

Look at the pictures on these pages. Listen.
What can you hear? Make a list.

Is each thing good or bad for the environment, do you think? Why?

Green Earth   Spring Issue

PEOPLE *and* PLANET EARTH

Problems for the environment

The Earth is 4,600 million years old. Modern man has lived on the Earth for only 35,000 years but, in that time, we have changed our planet in many ways. Many of the things that we have done are good, but many, many more are not good for the Earth.

Traffic pollution   In big cities, cars and buses have polluted the air. Many people in cities now have very bad health problems.

Factory pollution   Factories have also polluted the land and the water. As a result, many rivers and lakes are now dead.

The ozone layer   Around the Earth, there is a special type of oxygen called 'ozone' (O_3). Ozone is important because it stops ultraviolet radiation from the sun. Many aerosol sprays and factories destroy ozone and they have made a very big hole in the ozone layer. This means that too much ultraviolet radiation now enters Earth. This is very dangerous because it can cause cancer.

More carbon dioxide
Carbon dioxide (CO_2) in the air has increased a lot. (CO_2 comes from burning oil, coal and wood.) This has formed a 'blanket' around the Earth. The heat from the sun cannot escape and so the temperature is rising (the 'greenhouse effect'). This means that the level of the sea is rising and the climate is changing.

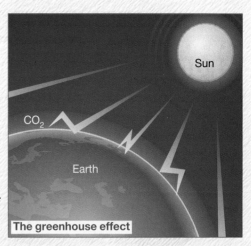
The greenhouse effect

Fewer trees   All over the world, people have cut down millions and millions of trees. As a result, many types of animals and plants are now disappearing. Trees are also important because they help to produce oxygen and control the climate.

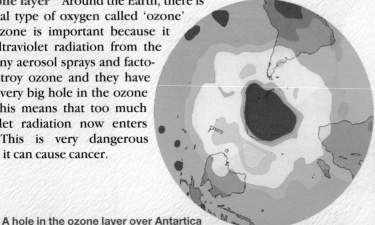
A hole in the ozone layer over Antartica

Deforestation

2 People and planet Earth

2.1 Some important concepts

Find the words in the article.

pollution   the ozone layer   the greenhouse effect

What does the article say about them? Tell the class.

2.2 What have we done?

Read the article and then work with a partner.
Copy and complete the chart below with information from the article.

What has happened?	What is the result?
Cars and buses have polluted the air.	Many people now have health problems.

Compare your notes with other students.

You can listen to the article on the cassette.

A wind generator

Hope for the future

These problems are very serious for our future, but we *can* do something *now!* In many places, they have already taken action to improve the environment. Many countries now use the wind, the sun and the sea to make electricity.

An electric car

In some cities, for example, you cannot drive your car on certain days. In other places they use electric cars and buses. There are also many other things we can do. To reduce traffic pollution, we can

red...
The
ren...
ar...
pol...

Inside the text

A Check your understanding

Are these sentences true or false?

1 The Earth is 35,000 years old.
2 Ozone protects us from the sun.
3 The temperature of the Earth is rising.

Write your answers to these questions.

1 Why are trees important?
2 What is ozone?
3 What is 'the greenhouse effect'?

Check your answers with your teacher. Then write some true/false sentences and some questions for other students.

B Linking ideas

Look how these ideas link together.

Modern man has lived on the Earth for only 35,000 years but, in that time, we have changed our planet in many ways.

Find these phrases in the article.
What do the words *like this* link to?

1 *This* means that too much ultraviolet radiation …
2 *This* is very dangerous …
3 *This* has formed a 'blanket' …
4 *This* means that the level of the sea …
5 … *they* help to produce …
6 *These* problems are very serious …

2.3 What can we do?

Look at the article again. What can we do about each problem? With your partner, make some notes. Compare ideas with the rest of the class.

Traffic pollution We can …

Use your notes to continue the article.

To reduce traffic pollution, we can …

3 Language focus **Present perfect**

3.1 **What do you say?**

How do you say these sentences in your language?

Cars and buses have polluted the air.
Aerosol sprays have made a hole in the ozone layer.

These sentences are examples of the Present perfect. You can use the Present perfect to talk about an action *in the past that has a result now*. For example:

Past action	Present result
Cars and buses have polluted the air.	Many people now have health problems.
Aerosol sprays have made a hole in the ozone layer.	Too much ultraviolet radiation now enters Earth.

Look at Exercise 2.2 again. What other examples of 'past action – present result' are there?
Can you match these past actions to the correct result?

Past action	Present result
I have done my homework …	… so we can eat it now.
I have studied English for ten years …	… so I know a lot of words.
My brother has made a cake …	… so I can watch TV now.

Think of some present results for these past actions.

I have walked 30 kilometres today so …   I have studied a lot of English today so …

Note: if you say a definite time, use the Past simple:

Yesterday, I walked 30 kilometres.   I did my homework last night.

3.2 **How to form the Present perfect**

The Present perfect has two main parts.

	have/has	+	past participle	
I	have		made	a cake.
I	have		done	my homework.
My brother	has		studied	English for ten years.
My friend	has		arrived.	

Words like 'made', 'done', 'studied' and 'arrived' are past participles.
'Studied' and 'arrived' are *regular* past participles, because they end in *-ed*.
'Made' and 'done' are *irregular*. Can you find them in the list on page 90?
Each verb has three parts. Look at the list and complete this table.

Infinitive ('dictionary form')	Past simple (Yesterday, last year, etc.)	Past participle (have/has +)
be	was, were	....
break	....	....
cut	....	....
....	....	done
eat	....	....
....	....	made
see	....	....

3.3 What have they done?

Work in pairs. Ask each other about the picture.

What has she done?   She's …
What have they done? They've …

Write five sentences about the people in the picture.

3.4 Experiences

You can use the Present perfect to talk about people's experiences. Work in pairs or in a small group. Ask each other some questions. You can answer:

No, I haven't.   or   Yes, I have.

and say when. (Be careful! Use the Past simple.) For example:

Have you ever eaten snake meat? – Yes, I have. I ate it yesterday!
Have you ever been to America? – Yes, I have. I went last year.

Have you ever walked 50 kilometres?
Have you ever seen a famous person?
Have you ever climbed a mountain?
Have you ever broken an arm or a leg?
Have you ever eaten chicken-flavoured ice-cream?
Have you ever written a letter in English?
Have you ever won a prize?
Have you ever swum 1 kilometre?
Have you ever been to a pop concert?

4 Alternative energy

Listen to part of 'Alternatives for tomorrow', a radio programme. Margareta Lindell is talking about alternative energy. Make a list of the problems she talks about. Compare your list with other students in your class.

Solar cells   Wave generator   Wind generator

Green Earth   Issue 53

Wave generators use the movement of the sea.

Solar cells make electricity from the sun.

Wind generators use the wind.

5 Your Language Record

5.1 Your Grammar Record

Make notes about the Present perfect in your *Grammar Record*.
Make notes about how to form it and how to use it. Look at Exercise
3 and the Language summaries in your Workbook for ideas.

5.2 Your Record of Language Use

Look back at Unit 7. Are there more words and phrases you want to add to your *Record of Language Use?*

Check your record with this list.

Nouns acid rain aerosol spray blanket environment generator greenhouse effect magnet manure ozone layer pipe pollution rubbish ultraviolet radiation

Verbs burn cause destroy escape increase mix pollute produce reduce turn

Time to spare?
Choose one of these exercises.

1 Look at the *Help yourself list* on page 91. Make an exercise about this Unit.

2 Write your answers to these questions. For example:

Have you ever been to the cinema?
Yes, I have. I went last Thursday.
Have you ever seen a shark?
Have you ever had a pet?
Have you ever run all the way to school?
Have you ever read a book in English?
Have you ever been in a helicopter?
Have you ever been on a boat?

3 Look at the extract about 'Transport for the 21st century' again. Can you invent a new type of transport? Draw a picture and explain how it works. You could use the wind, the sun, water, the sea, animal power, battery power.

Ecology;
curriculum links
with Environmental
Science; Future
simple; first
conditional

1 *Discussion*
2 *Brainstorming
and reading*
WB Ex. 1

3 *Reading and
writing*

8 Save the Earth!
Topic and language

1 Helping the environment

Look at the photographs. What are the people doing? Why? Tell the class your ideas.

Can you think of other ways to help the environment?

2 Think of the future

2.1 The way we live

The people in the photographs think that we need to change the way we live. Why? What problems do we make for the environment now? Work in a small group and brainstorm your ideas. Compare your ideas with the rest of the class.

We have too many cars.

THE WAY WE LIVE

We use too much water.

Green Earth Issue 53

Think of the future!

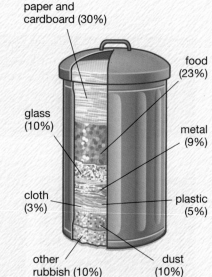

The population of the world is growing very fast. In the last 40 years, it has doubled. By the year 2200, it will be about 10,000 million. Our cities will be much bigger. There will be more factories and more roads. We will need more water and more natural resources. Experts say that we will have serious problems in the future. They say that we must change the way we use energy and natural resources NOW.

Recycle it!

Every day we throw away millions of tonnes of rubbish. Half of this is paper that we can use again. A typical family in Europe or America throws away more than 1 tonne of rubbish each year, but we can recycle most of this. If we recycle things, we can save money, energy and natural resources. Recycling the Sunday *New York Times* newspaper, for example, will save 75,000 trees every week.

paper and cardboard (30%)
food (23%)
glass (10%)
metal (9%)
cloth (3%)
plastic (5%)
other rubbish (10%)
dust (10%)

2.2 Some important words

Find these words in the article.

> natural resources   rubbish   recycle
> biodegradable   packaging   renewable

What does the article say about them? Tell the class.

2.3 Reasons to help the environment

Work in a group of three. Read paragraph one of the article and then each choose a different section to read ('Recycle it!', 'Reduce it!' or 'Save it!'). Tell each other what your part says. What reasons does the article give for changing the way we live?

You can listen to the article on the cassette.

Reduce it!

A lot of the rubbish that we throw away is not biodegradable. Plastic, metals and chemicals will not disappear for hundreds of years. We also produce a lot of unnecessary things, such as packaging. All of this pollutes the air, the land and the water. Pollution will be a very big problem in the future. We must avoid using non-biodegradable material. We must also reduce the amount of unnecessary things that we produce and use. In shops, for example, we can say 'No, thanks!' to the packaging that comes with the things we buy.

Save it!

Many natural resources are not renewable. Coal, gas, oil, metals and minerals, for example, will finish one day. Other resources take a long time to grow, such as trees, or they are not always available, such as water. We have to reduce the amount of resources and energy that we use. We also have to find alternative ways to make energy. We can use the sun, the wind, the sea and the heat of the Earth.

3 Recycle it, save it, reduce it ... but how?

Look at the picture of the house in the article. Can you match these sentences to the correct part of the picture?

1 Cover all saucepans when you are cooking.

2 Reduce packaging. Don't buy disposable bottles or boxes.

3 Save electricity. Turn off the lights when you are not using them.

4 Recycle boxes and plastic bottles.

5 Grow your own fruit and vegetables.

6 Save energy and natural materials. Recycle old clothes. Give them to a friend.

There are four more ideas in the picture. Write one or two sentences about each one.

4 Language focus Future simple

4.1 Life in the future

In Book 2, you saw 'going to' to talk about future plans.

I'm going to the cinema tomorrow.

Often, when we talk about future predictions we use 'will'.

By the year 2200, the population will be 10,000 million. There will be more factories and more roads.

You can use 'will' for everybody. The negative is 'won't' (will not).

I You He, She, It We You They	will need more water. will use more natural resources. will live in bigger cities. won't live in small villages. won't eat fresh fruit.

4.2 What do you think?

Experts say our cities will be much bigger in the future. They say there will be more factories and more roads. But how will we live? Tell the class your ideas.

We will work in…
We will drink…
We will communicate by…
Our houses will be…
OUR FUTURE
We will travel by…
People will…
We will eat…
We will live in…

4.3 100 years from now

Our lives will be very different in 2100. Read these ideas. Do you agree? Can you match them to the correct pictures a–g?

1 Everybody will live in very tall buildings.
2 We will travel in different ways.
3 Our cities will be much bigger.
4 We will eat very different food.
5 Plants and crops will be very different.
6 People will look very different.
7 The Earth will look very different.

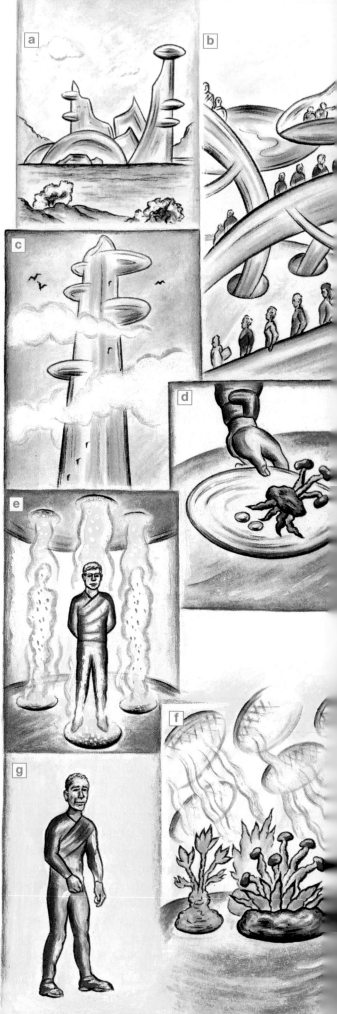

5 Language focus **First conditional**

Many of the ideas in Exercise 4.3 will happen if we don't change our lives now. Can you complete the sequence in the jigsaw puzzle?

If carbon dioxide (CO_2) in the air increases, the temperature will rise a lot.

If the ice melts, the sea level will rise.

If a lot of land disappears, people will have to move.

If the temperature rises, the ice at the poles will melt.

If the people have to move, our cities will become larger.

If the sea level rises, a lot of land will disappear.

If the climate changes, the winds and rain will also change. Can you write about what will happen?

If the climate changes, the winds and rain will change.
If the winds and rain change, plants and crops ...
If plants and crops ...

6 Think!

Work in pairs. Choose one of these questions and write about what you think will happen. Look at Exercise 5 for ideas.

What will happen if we don't have enough water in the future?

What will happen if the air is not good outside?

What will happen if there are too many cars?

What will happen if we don't have any coal, gas or oil?

What will happen if everybody works at home?

What will happen if cities grow to 100 million people?

Compare your ideas with other students.

7 Your Language Record

7.1 Your Grammar Record

Make notes about the Future simple and the First conditional in your *Grammar Record*. Make notes about how to form it and how to use it. Look at Exercises 4 and 5 and the Language summaries in your Workbook for ideas.

7.2 Your Record of Language Use

Look back at Unit 8. Are there more words and phrases you can add to your *Record of Language Use*? Check your record with this list.

Nouns city coal energy factory gas heat metal mineral natural resources oil packaging paper population rubbish

Adjectives biodegradable non-biodegradable unnecessary

Verbs disappear double recycle save reduce

Time to spare?

Choose one of these exercises.

1 Look at the *Help yourself list* on page 91. Make an exercise about this Unit.

2 Design a poster to tell people how they can help the environment.

3 Look at the article on pages 34–35 again. Find these words. What do they link to?

Paragraph 1: ... it will be ... They say ...
Paragraph 2: Half of this ... ... most of this
Paragraph 3: All of this ...

9 Whose is it?
Out and about with English

1 What do you think?

Discuss these questions with your class.

If you find something, does it belong to you?
Does it depend on what it is? Does it depend on
where you find it?

What do you think you should do if you find:

a a cheap watch in the street?
b a pen on the floor in your classroom?
c a bag full of school books in the park?
d a coin in the street?
e an expensive camera in a restaurant?
f some money on the floor at home?

2 Lost property

2.1 It's mine!

Listen to Blake and Samantha. What did
Samantha find? Why does she think it is hers
now? What do you think?

BLAKE: Hi, Samantha. You look happy.
SAMANTHA: Hello, Blake. I am! Look what I've found!
BLAKE: Five pounds! Where did you find that?

SAMANTHA: In the library. I was looking for something for my project about Canada. I found it inside an old book.
BLAKE: You should give it to a teacher.
SAMANTHA: What?! Why? I found it. It's mine. I don't have to give it to anybody.
BLAKE: It's not yours, Samantha. Someone put it there and they forgot it. You have to give it to a teacher.
SAMANTHA: Well, I don't think so. I think it's mine now. The last time someone borrowed that book was in 1994! I'm sure someone put it in there ages ago.
BLAKE: That doesn't matter, Samantha. You didn't put it there. It's not yours.
SAMANTHA: Yes, it is. If I give it to the teachers, what can they do with it?
BLAKE: I don't know. They can ask who put it there.
SAMANTHA: Oh, yes! Very clever! Everybody in the school will say that it's theirs. It's mine, Blake.

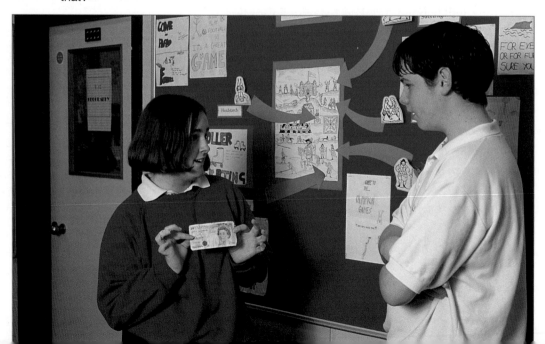

2.2 With a teacher

🔊 Listen again. What does Rebecca think about the money? What should Samantha tell Mrs Wilson? What do you think Mrs Wilson should do?

REBECCA: Hi, you two. What are you arguing about?

SAMANTHA: Nothing.

BLAKE: Samantha found five pounds in the library. I think that she should give it to the teachers but she says she doesn't have to. What do you think, Becky?

REBECCA: Well, …

SAMANTHA: Listen, you two. It was inside an old book that nobody reads. It's mine. I don't want to talk about it anymore.

REBECCA: Well, I think she's right, Blake. Five pounds isn't a lot of money.

BLAKE: Yes, it is! Anyway, it's the principle that is important.

SAMANTHA: Forget it, Blake. Come on, Becky, let's go outside. I can buy a drink for us.

BLAKE: Samantha! You mustn't spend it.

REBECCA: Wait a minute, Samantha. Wasn't Ester crying last week because she lost some money? Perhaps it belongs to her.

MRS WILSON: Hello, you three. What are you talking about?

SAMANTHA: Nothing, Miss. We're going outside.

BLAKE: Tell her, Samantha. Let Mrs Wilson decide.

MRS WILSON: Decide what, Blake? Samantha?

SAMANTHA: Er …

3 Inside the text

Look back through the dialogue in Exercise 2.

How many examples of 'should', 'have to', and 'mustn't' can you find? Add the examples to your *Record of Language Use*.

Samantha says 'It's mine!' Blake says 'It's not yours'. Can you find more words like 'mine' and 'yours'?

4 Decide …

Work by yourself or in a small group. Choose an exercise.

4.1 What happened next?

What happened in the end? Did Samantha keep the money? Prepare a conversation with Mrs Wilson. For example:

Mrs Wilson with Samantha, Blake and Rebecca
Mrs Wilson with Samantha
Mrs Wilson with Ester

Act out your conversation for the class.

4.2 Samantha's diary

What does Samantha think about what happened, do you think? Is she angry with Blake? Do you think she is still friends with Blake? Write Samantha's diary for the day.

Read your diary out to the class.

> *Thursday*
> *Today was a good day and a bad day. I was looking at some books in the library when…*

4.3 You decide!

Look at page 91 for ideas. You could also:

– write about when you lost something.
– write a poem about losing something.
– write a song about losing something. Choose a song you know and write some new words. Sing it!

Work by yourself. Answer the questions in the questionnaire.

Discuss your answers with other students in your class. How can you check your work more carefully?

Questionnaire
Checking your work

1 **After you have finished some written work, what do you do?**
- ☐ I close my book and put my paper away.
- ☐ I look at it again quickly.
- ☐ I read it all again slowly and carefully.
- ☐ I check it against my other work.
- ☐ I check it against a 'list of common mistakes'.
- ☐ Something else:

2 **Do you ever ask someone else to look at your work?**
- ☐ Always.
- ☐ Usually.
- ☐ Sometimes.
- ☐ Almost never.

3 **If you ask someone else to look at your work, who do you ask?**
- ☐ your teacher
- ☐ other students
- ☐ someone in your family
- ☐ someone else:

4 **When you get work back from the teacher, what do you do?**
- ☐ I look at the grade and put my paper away.
- ☐ I look carefully to see what I got wrong.
- ☐ I try to discover *why* I got something wrong.
- ☐ I make a note of the mistakes I made.
- ☐ Something else:

By yourself, look at Units 7–9 and find some written work which you gave to your teacher. How did you check it before you gave it to your teacher? What other ways could you check your work while you are writing? What did you do when you had the work back from the teacher? Compare your ideas with your partner or in a small group.

The world of music

1 Music in your country

What types of music do people listen to in your country? Do different types of music appeal to different groups of people? For example young people, older people, men, women.

What traditional music do people play in your country? Where does it come from? What instruments do they play? Is traditional music growing or disappearing, do you think?

2 A music school

2.1 A course you would like

Look at the leaflet about the music summer school. Which course would you like to do? Why? What other courses could they have in the summer school?

2.2 Find the pictures.

Look at Units 10-12. Can you find the pictures? What can you learn about in each unit?

AROUND THE THEME

SUMMER SCHOOL OF MUSIC

Courses on offer this year

For details of prices, course duration and registration see the back of this leaflet.

STUDIO EDITING

An introduction to basic editing techniques. During the course we will visit a recording studio and learn how recordings are made.

MUSIC AND COMPUTERS

Learn how you can use a computer to make and edit music. You will learn a wide range of techniques for special effects, from simple ones to more complex ones.

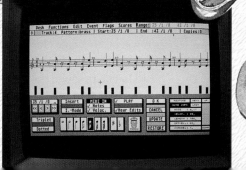

A HISTORY OF ROCK MUSIC

This course traces the history of popular music from the 'rhythm and blues' to new styles such as Afro-rock, rap, techno, and so on. You will learn about the different influences on music today.

INDIAN MUSIC

In this course, you can learn about the many different styles of Indian music, particularly sitar music and the raga.

MUSICAL APPRECIATION

This course covers a wide variety of types of music, and will help you to understand and appreciate music. You can learn about the structure of different types of music, including 'classical' music, jazz, blues, pop, and rock.

INSTRUMENTAL TUITION

Once again, this year you can learn the instrument of your choice. We have classes for beginners right up to more advanced levels in guitar, piano, flute, violin, harp, and many others. Ring and ask for the latest details.

10 The sound of music
Topic and language

1 Music all around us

1.1 Music and you

Read these questions. Tell the class what you think.

What type of music do you like?
What type of music don't you like?
Who are your favourite musicians?
Do you ever buy cassettes or CDs?
How has your taste in music changed?

1.2 Musical instruments

Do you play a musical instrument? What instrument would you like to play?

Can you match the correct name to the pictures? Some of the instruments come from particular countries. Do you know where?

balalaika   drums   harp   school recorder
violin   flute   sitar   pipes   piano   trumpet
guitar   synthesiser

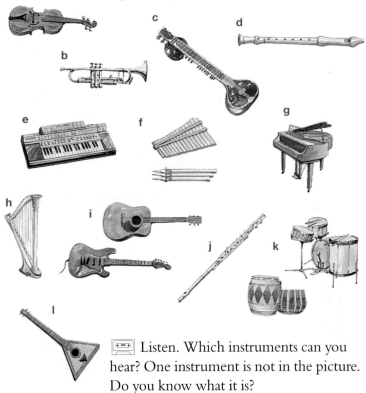

📼 Listen. Which instruments can you hear? One instrument is not in the picture. Do you know what it is?

1.3 Music from around the world

📼 Listen to some pieces of music from different countries. Can you guess where they are from? What type of instruments can you hear?

A (very short) history of

Rock music in one form or another is now the most popular type of music all over the world. But where did it come from?

BLACK MUSIC

Rock began in the USA in the early 1950s. At that time, 'rhythm and blues' music was very popular with black Americans. 'R & B' was a mixture of black religious music ('gospel') and jazz. It had strong rhythms that you could dance to and simple, fast lyrics.

ROCK 'N' ROLL

Noticing the success of R & B music, white musicians started to copy the same style. By the mid 1950s, this new white R & B music, called 'rock 'n' roll', had become very popular. Singers like Elvis Presley and Bill Haley attracted millions of teenage fans. Their music was fast and loud. Many older people thought that rock 'n' roll was very dangerous.

By the early 1960s, even rock 'n' roll had become old-fashioned. Many of the songs had begun to sound the same. It was at that time that a new group from England became popular: The Beatles.

2 A (very short) history of rock music

2.1 Musical pictures

One type of music that is popular all over the world is rock music. Look at the pictures in the article. Do you know the names of any groups like those? Do you like their music?

2.2 Types of rock

Do you know what these musical labels mean? Compare ideas with other people in your class.

R & B   gospel   rock 'n' roll   rock   reggae   rap   disco

📼 Now read and listen to a (very short) history of rock music. Check your ideas. Can you explain each label?

ROCK MUSIC

THE BEATLES

The Beatles first started by singing American style songs, but they soon developed their own style, with more complicated melodies. They also introduced different instruments, such as the Indian sitar. Groups like The Beatles had a very important influence on the style of popular music.
By the early 1970s, rock 'n' roll had developed into a new form of music. Electronics had replaced the amplified guitars and drums of rock 'n' roll. 'Rock' had arrived.

ROCK TODAY

Rock music has continued to change and develop. It has combined with music from different parts of the world. Today, there are hundreds of different types of rock music, and almost every country has its own form of rock. There is 'heavy metal' which is extremely loud with hard rhythms, 'reggae', from Jamaica, that combines rock with jazz and Latin rhythms, 'rap' that developed on the streets of New York, 'disco' a type of soft rock music for dancing, 'Afro-rock' that combines rock with African rhythms, 'Mex-rock', which combines rock with traditional Mexican melodies … and many, many more.

Inside the text

A What does it mean?

Can you match the words in Box 1 with the words in Box 2?

1

the early 1950s	old-fashioned
the mid 1950s	such as
mixture	replace
lyrics	combine
popular	develop

2

different things	1954, 1955, 1956 …
together	many people like it
for example	take the place of
grow	something
join together	the words of a song
out of date	1951, 1952, 1953 …

B Check your understanding

Work in pairs. Student A can read *Black music* and *Rock 'n' roll*, Student B can read *The Beatles* and *Rock today*.
Make notes about the following things. Then tell your partner what the text says.

Student A	**Student B**
The early 1950s	The Beatles
The mid 1950s	The early 1970s
The early 1960s	Rock music today

3 Language focus Past perfect

3.1 What's it for?

In Units 7 and 8 you saw sentences with the Present perfect:

> I have done my homework …
>> … so I can watch TV now.
> I have studied English for 10 years …
>> … so I know a lot of words.

Do you remember what we use the Present perfect for? (Hint: past action, present result)

In Exercise 2.1 you saw sentences with the Past perfect. For example:

> By the mid 1950s, 'rock 'n' roll' <u>had become</u> very popular.
> By the beginning of the 1960s, rock 'n' roll <u>had become</u> old-fashioned.
> Many of the songs <u>had begun</u> to sound the same.

How do you say those sentences in your language? What do you think we use the Past perfect for? Tell the class your ideas.

3.2 How to form the Past perfect

Here are some more examples of the Past perfect. How can you describe it? (Look at page 32 for ideas.)

> They found one of Franklin's sailors in 1857, but he <u>had died</u> ten years earlier.
> People say Europeans discovered Australia, but the Aborigines <u>had discovered</u> it 12,000 years earlier.
> The *Hindenburg* <u>had made</u> ten trips before it exploded in 1937.

3.3 PRACTICE

Read more about The Beatles and complete the text with the Past perfect. (Use the list of verbs on page 90 to help you.)

1 play	6 record
2 become	7 sell
3 change	8 make
4 introduce	9 win
5 experiment	

▭ Listen and check your answers.

A (very short) history of THE BEATLES

The Beatles were probably the most important pop and rock group of all time.
They were together for only eight years, but their influence has lasted much longer.

The Beatles came from Liverpool, England. They started playing together in 1962, although Paul McCartney and John Lennon ……… 1 ……… together in another group. They started by playing rock 'n' roll songs, but they quickly developed their own style. By 1963, they ……… 2 ……… Britain's top rock group. A year later they toured the United States, where they attracted millions of fans.

By the time The Beatles broke up in 1970, they ……… 3 ……… the nature of rock and pop music. They ……… 4 ……… new sounds and rhythms, and they ……… 5 ……… with different types of musical instruments. They ……… 6 ……… hundreds of songs and they ……… 7 ……… millions and millions of records. They ……… 8 ……… many films and ……… 9 ……… many awards for their music.

Today, Beatles songs are still very famous all over the world.

3.4 Stolen!

Look at this picture of a rock group's recording studio. When their manager arrived this morning, he found that thieves had got into the studio. What had they done? Write eight sentences about the picture.

They had broken ... They had ...

The rock group doesn't believe their manager. They think *he* stole their guitars and drums. Why do they think that? Look carefully at the picture!

WE HAVE YOUR GUITARS AND DRUMS!

4 Your Language Record

4.1 You Grammar Record

Make notes about the Past perfect in your *Grammar Record*. Make notes about how to form it and how to use it. Look at Exercise 3 and the Language summaries in your Workbook for ideas.

4.2 You Record of Language Use

Look at Unit 10. Are there more words you can add to your *Record of Language Use*? Check your record with this list.

Verbs attract develop introduce replace combine last break up experiment record take (time) mix analyse

Nouns guitar drums violin trumpet flute balalaika pipes sitar harp piano recorder synthesiser mixture rhythm lyrics style melody influence award record profile

Adjectives popular early (1950s, etc.) religious teenage old-fashioned complicated amplified loud hard soft live

Time to spare?

Choose one of these exercises.

1 Look at the *Help yourself list* on page 91. Make an exercise about this Unit.

2 Think of a song that you like. Write some new words in English about your class, your school or your town.

3 Before your English lesson started, what had you done? Write a few sentences.

We had had a Maths lesson. We had learned about ...

FOCUS ON
The music industry

1 The world of music

1.1 Search!

Look at the texts. Can you find answers to these questions?

a Which texts are about technology? Which texts are about business?
b When did compact discs first appear?
c What is another word for 'group'?
d How long does it take to record a new CD or cassette?
e Why have some rock groups started their own record companies?

Write some more 'search' questions for other students.

1.2 Read and think

Read *New technology: Singing ghosts?*. What will happen to jobs in recording studios and the work of a singer?

Read *What next?*. Can you think of a similar problem with other new technology? (Hint: cameras, TVs, radios, motor cars …)

Read *In the studio*. Sometimes a rock or pop group makes a 'remix' of their songs. What do you think that is?

Read *Music is big business*. Find eight examples of the word 'they'. Who is 'they' in each sentence?

In the studio

In the 1960s, it took pop and rock groups one or two days to record their songs. Nowadays, it can take months and months. Many rock groups begin by recording only one instrument, for example, the voice. Then, they record other instruments – electric piano, synthesiser, guitars, drums and so on.

Next, they might use a computer to add special effects. Finally, they 'mix' all the instruments until they get the sound that they want. This means that a CD or cassette will always sound very different from a live concert.

Music is big business

Most of us listen to music for pleasure, but for the record companies, music is a product, the same as soap powder. When a record company finds a new group (or 'band'), they first try to develop the band's 'profile'. They will try to create an 'image' for the band, that they think will attract young people. They will often tell the band what they should wear, what they should say and how they should sing and play.

In recent years, many rock groups have started their own record companies because they say that the big companies are too commercial.

2 Decide ...

Choose **a** or **b**.

a Work in pairs. Imagine ...

You are on a radio programme called 'Music today'. One of you is an interviewer, the other is an 'expert'. Use the information in the texts or any information you have.

INTERVIEWER: Prepare some questions about music today. You can ask about the new computer program, the history of disc players, the music industry ... and more.

EXPERT: Read through the information and make some notes.

When you are ready, practise your interview together. Then, act it out for the class.

b You decide!

Decide what *you* want to do and ask your teacher. You could:

– write about your favourite pop or rock group or singer.
– write about a musical instrument that you play.
– think of a song and write some new words.
– write an interview with a musician.

Look at the *Help yourself list* on page 91 for ideas.

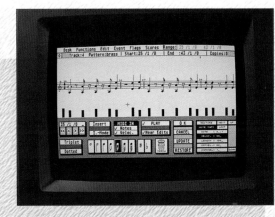

New technology: Singing ghosts?

Music engineers have developed a new computer programme that will change the future of music. A computer can analyse a singer's voice. Then, if you give the computer the lyrics and music of a song, the computer can 'sing' it in that voice. This means that a singer only needs to record one song and the computer can then sing other songs in the singer's own voice. Singers can sing new songs many years after they have died.

1878

1900

1930

1952

1964

What next?

Technology is changing very fast. A new way of playing recorded music appears every few years. For most of us, this is a big problem. Very soon, it will be impossible to play the discs and cassettes that we have at home. For the record industry, this is a big advantage.

When compact discs appeared in 1983, for example, many record companies produced all their old recordings again.

New technology is new business. Sony, for example, owns a recording company and makes compact discs and compact disc players, so it is in their interest to develop new technology.

1983

1987

1993

2000+

12 Revision

1 How well do you know it?

How well do you think you know the English you learnt in units 10–11? Put a tick (√) in the table

Now choose some sections to revise and practise.

	very well	*OK*	*a little*
New vocabulary			
Present perfect (have done)			
Future simple (will do)			
Offers (I'll …)			
Past perfect (had done)			

2 A puzzle

Write the words from the clues in the puzzle.

```
1 [ ][ ][ ][N][ ][ ]
      2 [A][ ][ ][ ][ ][ ]
      3 [T][ ][ ][ ][ ][ ][ ][ ]
   4 [U][ ][ ]
      5 [R][ ][ ][ ][ ]
    6 [A][ ][ ][ ][ ][ ]
  7 [L][ ][ ]

        8 [R][ ][ ][ ][ ]
        9 [E][ ][ ][ ][ ]
  10 [ ][S][ ][ ]
  11 [ ][O][ ][ ][ ][ ][ ][ ][ ][ ]
12 [ ][U][ ][ ][ ]
  13 [ ][R][ ][ ][ ][ ]
      14 [C][ ][ ][ ]
15 [ ][E][ ][ ][ ][ ]
      16 [S][ ][ ][ ]
```

1 A special type of oxygen around the Earth.
2 A..................... sprays pollute the air.
3 In the last 100 years, the t..................... of the Earth has risen almost 1°C.
4 Every day, we produce millions of tonnes of r......................
5 We must try to r..................... the amount of energy that we use.
6 The paper and plastic that comes with the things that we buy.
7 Scientists have discovered a h..................... in the ozone layer.
8 We can r..................... many of the things we use. For example, we can use paper again.
9 The temperature of the Earth is rising because of 'the greenhouse e.....................'.
10 Oxygen is a g......................
11 Plastic is not b...................... It will not disappear for hundreds of years.
12 In most big cities, there is a lot of p......................
13 If you burn coal and oil, you get c..................... dioxide.
14 A black mineral that we can burn.
15 Many of our natural resources are not r......................
16 We have to s..................... energy.

3 School news

3.1 The week at school

Read the text and choose the correct phrase for each gap.

have collected have cleaned
have collected have done
have designed have found
have lost have organised
have put have taken

3.2 What has happened?

What has happened in your school this week? Write five sentences. For example:

This week, we have had a test. We have watched a video. We have …

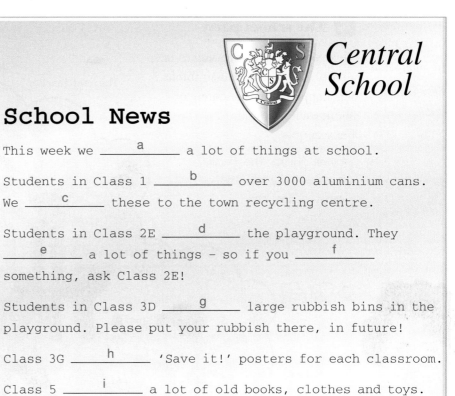

Central School

School News

This week we _____a_____ a lot of things at school.

Students in Class 1 _____b_____ over 3000 aluminium cans. We _____c_____ these to the town recycling centre.

Students in Class 2E _____d_____ the playground. They _____e_____ a lot of things - so if you _____f_____ something, ask Class 2E!

Students in Class 3D _____g_____ large rubbish bins in the playground. Please put your rubbish there, in future!

Class 3G _____h_____ 'Save it!' posters for each classroom.

Class 5 _____i_____ a lot of old books, clothes and toys. They are going to have a sale on 17th March. Please come!

We _____j_____ another meeting on 20th March. Please come with more ideas.

3.3 When do you use the Present perfect?

Exercises 3.1 and 3.2 have many examples of the Present perfect.
When can you use the Present perfect? Choose an answer.

You can use the Present perfect:
a when you want to talk about the future.
b when you want to talk about things that happened last week, yesterday, last year.
c when you want to talk about things that happened this week, today, this year and that have a result now.

Find some examples in Exercises 3.1 and 3.2 to prove your answer.

3.4 How many can you find?

How many participles can you find in the puzzle? How many are the same as the infinitive?

How many are the same as the Past simple?

How many are completely different?

Write some sentences using the past participles.

```
B E E N M A F A L L E N
N H Y D O N E W O K E N
S G K N O W N D R U N K
U O B N M X C R R U N M
N N H A D W R I T T E N
G E S A I D T O L D V D
C O M E R E A D S A T B
```

4 The school party

Next week, Class 3 is going to have a party. This is what Susan thinks will happen. Write a sentence about each person.
For example.

Susan thinks the head teacher will say the music is too loud.

5 What will happen?

Finish the sentences with your own words.

1 if we recycle all our paper ....
2 if we reduce the amount of packaging ....

....

3 if we don't use plastic bags ....
4 if we manufacture electric cars we will ....

6 I'll help!

You want to help these people.
What can you say? For example:

I'll carry your bag!

7 Music words

Can you find the word on the CD? (The end of each word is the beginning of the next word.)

1 'Gospel' is a type of black r............. music.
2 'R & B' music had strong r............. that you could dance to.
3 A lot of rock music is very l.............
4 A type of instrument from India.
5 A type of musical instrument that you blow.
6 A rock group's instruments are usually two or three guitars and a set of ....
7 It can t............. many months to record new songs.

8 Nowadays they often use e............. to make new sounds.
9 Rock groups r............. their songs in a studio.
10 The Beatles had an important influence on the s............. of popular music.
11 The Beatles were very p............. They sold millions of records.
12 The opposite of 'loud'.
13 The person who cuts and checks the recording in a studio.
14 To grow or change.

CD text: LOUDEVELOPOPULARECORDRUMSOFTRUMPETAKELECTRONICSTARELIGIOUSTYLEDITORHYTHM

8 It happened because ...

Can you match the two parts of these sentences?

1 My teacher was very angry with me yesterday because ...
2 Jack couldn't play the guitar because ...
3 I didn't see Jack at the party because ...
4 Steven knew the way to David's house because ...
5 Last summer, I didn't play football because ...
6 Last night I didn't have to do any homework because ...
7 Yesterday, I walked home from school because ...
8 I didn't go to the cinema with my friends because ...

a ... I had done it before.
b ... I had seen the film before.
c ... I had broken my leg.
d ... he had already left.
e ... he had forgotten his music.
f ... I had forgotten to take my bus money to school.
g ... he had been there before.
h ... I had forgotten to do my homework.

9 I had never done that before!

Tony has just come back from an unusual trip. What is he telling his friend? Write a sentence for each picture.

It was fantastic! I did so many things, I had never drunk from an oasis before. I had never ...

a *I had never drunk from an oasis before.*
b ....
c ....
d ....
e ....
f ....

Answer the questions in the questionnaire.

Discuss your answers with other students in your class.

How can you improve your memory?

Questionnaire
Memory

1 **What things do you find it easy to remember?**
 What things do you find it difficult to remember?

2 **What helps you to remember, do you think?**
 (Tick ✓ the techniques you have tried.)
 ❑ I study for a short time every day.
 ❑ I look back at my work every few days.
 ❑ I try to remember every evening all the things I learned that day.
 ❑ Something else:

3 **Which techniques have you tried to help you remember words?**
 (You can tick more than one.)

 ❑ I make notes.
 ❑ I record the words on a cassette.
 ❑ I put the new words into a story or song.
 ❑ I make a picture with all the new words.
 ❑ I tell someone else about the things I've learned.
 ❑ I write words/sentences on pieces of paper and stick them on the wall.
 ❑ I say words to myself while I am waiting somewhere.
 ❑ Something else:

4 **Do the techniques you have tried work well?**
 ❑ Always.
 ❑ Usually.
 ❑ Sometimes.
 ❑ Almost never.
 Why?

By yourself, look at Units 1–12. What language do you have problems remembering? What language do you remember very well? Why do you think that is? Compare your ideas with other students.

Theme E — Moving images

1 At the cinema

1.1 A good film

What 'good' films have you seen? Why are they 'good'? Have you seen any 'bad' films? Why are they 'bad'? Tell the class your ideas.

1.2 Important qualities?

What do you think makes a 'good' film? Work with a partner and brainstorm your ideas.

A GOOD FILM

How important is each thing? Give a point for each one: 0 = not important, 4 = very important. Compare with other students.

2 Take a look at Theme E

2.1 A trip to the cinema

Look at the advertisements. Imagine you could go to the cimema tonight. What film would you like to see? Why?

2.2 Find the pictures

Look at Units 13–14 and Optional Unit E. Where can you find the pictures in the advertisements? What are the units about?

ALL AROUND THE THEME

STAR MULTICINEMA

THE VAMPIRE

Midnight … the air is cold, the wind is still, and you are asleep in your bed. There's a noise at the window… Sean Vandibilt and Ursula Romani star in the story of horror… You'll never want to be alone again!

On a flight from Kenya, a plane crashes. Tess and Philip are the sole survivors. The love story of the 21st century.

AFRICAN SUN

Cliff Watson's latest western. Also starring: Derek Jackson, Deni Kass, Su Lee Han. The story of one man's search for gold.

A MAN AND HIS HORSE

Visitors from space

There is something in space that we don't know about. The year is 2100. On a routine flight to Mars, the passengers see something unusual. Is it the beginning of the end for Planet Earth?

MURDER IN THE NIGHT

Lena Gomez stars as Det Sgt Black in a spine-chilling story of murder

Krazy Kevin 3

Kevin is back! More cartoon fun for all the family

The cinema;
curriculum links
with Media
Studies and
Technical Design;
gerunds;
discourse
structure

1 *Discussion,*
listening
WB Ex. 1

2 *Writing*

3 *Reading*

13 The big screen
Topic and language

First
Meeting

romance

1 On the big screen

1.1 The films you like

Look at the pictures. What type of films do you like most?

What films have you seen recently? What were they about? Did you like them? Why/Why not? Tell the class your ideas.

western

A TEXAS COWBOY

MURDER

DON'T
WALK

IN THE NIGHT

detective

Spacewalk

science fiction

1.2 Music and film

🎴 Music is very important in a film. It helps to create an atmosphere. Listen. What type of film do you think each piece of music comes from?

2 A film review

2.1 A film you have seen

Think about a film you have seen. What was it about? What happened? Who was in it? What did you think about it? Work by yourself and make some notes. For example:

Spacewalk
– science fiction
– a space ship explodes
– three people can't get back from the moon

Use your notes to tell your neighbour about the film.

THE VAMPIRE

horror

2.2 A review poster

Use your notes to write a short description of the film. For example:

Spacewalk
Spacewalk is a science fiction film. In the film, some people go to the moon. Everything goes OK until they want to come back. Suddenly, …

Give the film one to five stars.

Put all your reviews together and make a poster for your class.

3 How do they make a film?

3.1 The people who make it

Usually, at the end of a film there is a long list of people who made it. Look at this list. Do you know what each person does?

the producer   the director   the writer
the editor

Tell the class your ideas.

3.2 The film-makers

Are you right? Read about the steps in making a film. Who is the most important person, do you think? Why? Who has the most interesting job? What job would you like to do? Why?

🎴 You can listen to the text on the cassette.

STEP 1: THE IDEA

A film starts with an idea. Often, this comes from **a producer** who is interested in making a particular type of film. The producer contacts a writer.

The writer writes a script. If the producer likes it, the producer then contacts a director.

The director plans how they can make the film. If the producer agrees, the director then chooses the people who will help to make the film.

STEP 2: MAKING THE FILM

The director decides exactly what will happen in each scene.

The director of special effects organises the special effects for the film.

The producer organises the money for the film and how the public will see it (e.g. in cinemas, television or on video).

The actors. Often, there are one or two main actors or actresses ('stars'), some supporting actors and 'extras' who appear in the crowd scenes.

The casting director has the job of choosing the actors.

The designers are responsible for choosing the clothes and the make-up for the actors, and for deciding what the 'set' will look like.

The director of photography is in charge of directing all the camera operators.

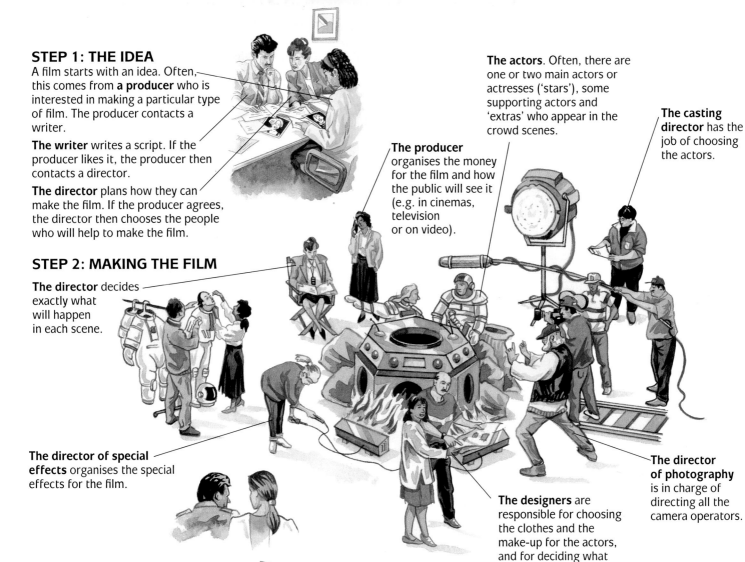

STEP 3: EDITING THE FILM

Every day, **the editors** produce film for the director to check. They cut the film and join it together the way the director wants it.

STEP 4: SELLING THE FILM

When the film is ready, the producer contacts the distributors.
The distributors sell the film to video shops, television companies and cinemas and we see it!

Inside the text

A Check your comprehension

What is the job title of these people?

1 A person who chooses the actors.
2 A person who arranges the finance.
3 A person who sells the film.
4 A person who decides what will happen in each scene.
5 A person who makes cuts in the film.
6 A person who controls the camera operators.

B What happens?

Look at these examples of the zero conditional.

If the producer likes it, the producer then contacts a director.

If the producer agrees, the director then chooses the people who will help to make the film.

Can you complete these sentences with your own ideas?

1 If the producer doesn't like the writer's script, …
2 If the film is too long, …
3 If the distributors do not promote the film, …
4 If a film is a great success, …
5 If a film is not very popular, …
6 If the film wins a prize, …

4 Language focus Gerunds

4.1 Verbs after prepositions

Words like *of, in, at, about, for, with, by, up, down* and *from* are called prepositions. Look at these sentences. How do you say them in your language? What do you notice about the form of the verb after a preposition?

> I'm not interested in seeing that film.
> They use a computer for editing the film.
> She's very good at acting.

Look back at the text in Exercise 3.2 and find more examples of a verb after a preposition.

4.2 PRACTICE

Read the story about Henry Brown. Underline the prepositions and then write the correct form of the verb.

A great film-maker?

Henry Brown was interested in ......a...... (make) a cowboy film. Unfortunately, he wasn't very good at ......b...... (convince) people to lend money to him. In the end, he only got the money to make the film by ......c...... (sell) his car. He was very unhappy about ......d...... (do) this, but there wasn't any other way. He didn't get a lot of money for his car so, instead of ......e...... (go) to Texas, he made the film in his house.

He saved a lot more money by ......f...... (act) in the film himself. He was also responsible for ......g...... (film) it, ...h...... (edit) it, and ......i...... (distribute) it. When the film was ready, Henry Brown took it to a cinema. Unfortunately, he was the only person who was interested in ......j...... (see) the film. He was afraid of ......k...... (lose) all his money, so he did a very clever thing. He got rid of all the tickets by ......l...... (sell) them to himself!

4.3 Verbs as nouns

You can also use the *-ing* form of verb like a noun. How do you say these sentences in your language?

> Making a film takes a long time.
> Acting is difficult.
> Editing a film is very complicated.

Make some more examples. Choose a topic from Box A and use a phrase from Box B to write some sentences that are true for you.

> **Box A**
> Learning English   Walking to school
> Swimming   Playing football   Reading
> Singing   Watching TV every day

> **Box B**
> is a good way to keep fit   is very easy
> is very difficult   is very dangerous
> is very boring   is very interesting
> takes a long time   is very enjoyable

5 Making a cartoon

5.1 How do they do it?

Listen to Frank Goodson, an artist. He is talking about how they make a cartoon. Can you put the pictures a–f in the correct order?

5.2 The process

Check your answers to Exercise 5.1. Can you write the correct picture letter by each sentence?

- [ ] First, they draw some pictures to show what will happen.
- [ ] Next, they draw the pictures for the background.
- [ ] Then, on transparent celluloid, they draw the pictures that will change.
- [ ] When they have drawn all the 'cels', they put one 'cel' on top of the background picture and take a photograph. They do this many times.
- [ ] Finally, in a recording studio they add music and dialogue.
- [ ] In the cinema or on television, you see the pictures very fast and hear the dialogue and music. Your brain thinks that the characters are really moving!

6 Language focus Explaining a process

Look at the text in Exercise 5.2 again. Notice how you can explain a process:

First, they …   Next, they …   Then, they …
When they have …, they …   Finally, …

Think of another process. Make some notes about how they do it. Then, using your notes tell your neighbour and the class. Some ideas:

How they record a pop or rock song
How they make a film
How they make electricity
How they make paper
How they build a house
How they make bread

7 Your Language Record

7.1 Your Grammar Record

Make notes about gerunds in your *Grammar Record*. Make notes about how to form sentences with gerunds after prepositions and gerunds as nouns. Look at the text in Exercise 3, Exercise 4 and the Language summaries in your Workbook for ideas.

7.2 Your Record of Language Use

Look back at Unit 13. Are there more words and phrases you can add to your *Record of Language Use*? Check your record with this list.

Nouns screen producer director writer editor designer special effects actor actress distributor public script operator background celluloid movement set (in a film) crowd scene

Verbs contact agree organise join something together convince get rid of something

Adjectives (types of films) western detective romance science fiction horror cartoon transparent

Adverbs first next then finally

Useful phrases has responsibility for has the job of in charge of is responsible for on top of

Time to spare?   Choose one of these exercises.

1 Look at the *Help yourself list* on page 91.
  Make an exercise about this Unit.

2 Look at Exercise 2 again. Write about a one-star or five-star film.
  Say what you didn't like or liked a lot about the film.

3 Draw a simple cartoon with five or six pictures. Write the dialogue.

Perception;
relative clauses;
curriculum links
with Science,
Psychology
and Art

14 Seeing is believing
Topic and language

1 What can you see?

Look at the picture. Put it close to your eyes and then slowly move the picture away from your eyes.

What can you see?

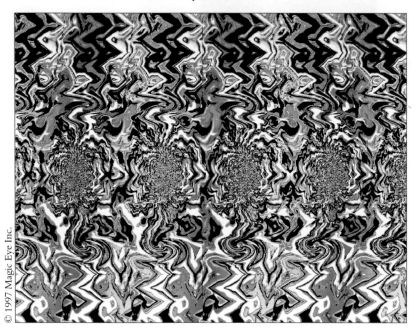

© 1997 Magic Eye Inc.

The answer can be seen on page 96.

2 The flying saucer story

Some years ago in the United States of America a man was flying in a plane when he suddenly saw ... a flying saucer! He took a lot of photographs before it suddenly disappeared. He sold the photographs to a newspaper and the government then started an investigation. Many months later they discovered what the man had seen.

What do you think he had seen?

▭ Are you right? Listen to the story and find out!

3 In the mind

3.1 Our eyes and our brain

Work with your neighbour. Read about how our brain helps us to see – and to see things that aren't really there.

One of you can read the introduction and paragraphs 1, 2 and 3. The other one can read the introduction and paragraphs 4 and 5.

Tell your neighbour what 'your' paragraphs say.

3.2 Things you don't understand

Now, with your neighbour, make a list of the words and phrases that you don't understand.

> <u>Things we don't understand</u>
> effective
> what is really there

Look carefully at the text again. Can you guess the meaning of the words? Compare your ideas with others in your class.

Can you believe your eyes?

Our eyes are not as effective as those of many other animals so we use our brain to help us understand what we see. This is called 'perception'. We do this in different ways.

❶ SEEING CAN BE MAKING MISTAKES

In order to understand what we see, we use our eyes and our brain. Sometimes, our brain misunderstands the message which comes from our eyes and we 'see' something different from what is really there. We call this an 'optical illusion'.

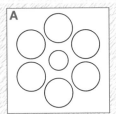
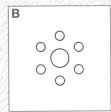

Look at the circles in the middle of each diagram. Is the middle circle in diagram A bigger than the middle circle in diagram B? Is this circle bigger in B than in A? Are they both the same size?

❷ SEEING IS MAKING DESIGNS

We find it easier to make patterns between shapes which are close together.

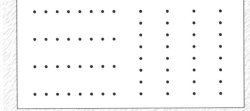

Look at the dots in the picture above. What do you see? Do the dots go down, across or diagonally? Look at the dots in the picture below. What kind of pattern do these dots make? Do they go down, across or diagonally?

❸ SEEING IS FILLING IN THE GAPS

When we read a sentence which has a word missing we try to guess what could be in the gap. In the same way, when we see only part of an object, we try to guess what the rest of the object is. Look at this picture. What object do you see? What can you guess?

❹ SEEING IS MAKING CONNECTIONS

When we see objects we try to make sense of them. When we look at patterns of dots or lines we like to find connections between them. Look at the seven lines in this picture. Do you see:
– seven unconnected lines?
– two groups of three lines and one line?
– a group of four lines and a group of three?
– three groups of two and one extra line?
– some other pattern?
Different people see the lines in different ways.

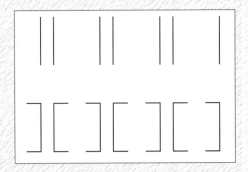

❺ TRICKS OF THE LIGHT

Sometimes, nature can trick our eyes. Mirages, which many people have seen, are another trick of the light. Mirages happen when light passes from hot air to cold air or from cold air to hot air. This bends the light and causes an object to appear much closer than it really is. People who travel in deserts often see mirages of water and trees.

A mirage in Antarctica

People who live in cold climates often see mirages of buildings. We can take photographs of mirages because the image is 'real'.

A mirage in Kenya

4 Language focus
Relative clauses (1)

4.1 One sentence, two ideas

How do you say these sentences in your language?

> People who travel in deserts often see mirages. Sometimes, our brain misunderstands the message which comes from our eyes.

These sentences have examples of 'relative clauses'. A relative clause gives you details about who or what the subject is. Look:

> People <u>who travel in deserts</u> often see mirages. Sometimes, our brain misunderstands the message <u>which comes from our eyes</u>.

Look at these sentences. Can you underline the relative clauses?

> People who are colour blind cannot see red and green very clearly.
> People who lose the sight of one eye can still see quite clearly.
> Many experiments which test perception are very well known.
> Usually the things which we notice first are the biggest and brightest things.

4.2 'who' or 'which'?

Look at the sentences in Exercise 4.1 again. Why do some have 'who' and some have 'which'? Discuss it with your neighbour and try to make a rule. Tell the class your ideas.

4.3 Test your rule

Can you match the correct relative clause (a–e) to each sentence?

1 The woman .... did not give her name.
2 The dictionary .... was not in the shop.
3 My friend .... now lives in the USA.
4 The classrooms .... are very noisy.
5 The students .... had to do extra homework.

a who used to live next door
b which are on the second floor
c who came late
d which I wanted to buy
e who phoned last night

5 Language focus
Relative clauses (2)

5.1 Brueghel's painting

Your teacher will give you some information to read about Brueghel's painting. When you have read it, look at the painting. What can you see? Write a few sentences.

The man who is carrying the food has a red hat.

5.2 We see what we expect to see

Some years ago, some scientists tried an experiment with Brueghel's painting. Read about what they did.

We see what we expect to see

In the experiment sixty people heard a story about a party. They were in two groups of thirty. The stories were different. They heard them on a cassette. One story said that the people in the party were happy. The other story said that the people in the party started fighting.

Next, the sixty people looked at a painting by Brueghel. The scientists told both groups of people that Brueghel had painted the picture about the party. The sixty people looked at the picture for only a few minutes. Then, they wrote about what they saw in the picture. The first group said that everybody in the picture was very happy. They had heard a story about a happy party. The second group said that everybody in the picture was fighting. They had heard a story about a fight at the party. The scientists had proved an important point: we see what we expect to see.

Did you see what you expected to see? Look back at your sentences from Exercise 5.1.

Look back at the text. You can make one sentence from each pair of coloured sentences. Like this:

> In the experiment sixty people heard a story about a party. They were in two groups of thirty.

> → In the experiment sixty people, who were in two groups of thirty, heard a story about a party.

Pieter Brueghel the Elder (1515–1569) *Peasant wedding*

Can you do the same with the other pairs of sentences? Remember, use 'who' for people and 'which' for things.

The stories, which they heard …
The first group, who heard …

6 Your Language Record

6.1 Your Grammar Record

Make notes about relative clauses with 'who' and 'which' in your *Grammar Record*. Make notes about how to form them and how to use them. Look at Exercises 4 and 5 and the Language summaries in your Workbook for ideas.

6.2 Your Record of Language Use

Look back at Unit 14. Are there more words and phrases you can add to your *Record of Language Use*? Check your record with this list.

Nouns flying saucer   investigation   brain   perception   message   optical illusion   diagram   pattern   object   mirage   trick

Adjectives effective   connected   unconnected

Verbs misunderstand   guess   make sense   trick   bend

Time to spare?

Choose one of these exercises.

1 Look at the *Help yourself list* on page 91. Make an exercise about this Unit.

2 Do you know any stories about people who have seen things that are not really there? Write about one.

3 Look at Brueghel's painting again. Write a short description. Do you like the painting? Why/why not?

Discussion about
fairness and
personal property

1 *Discussion*

2 *Listening*

3 *Language use*

4 *Decide …*

15 It's your fault
Out and about with English

1 What do you think?

Discuss these questions with your class.

If you borrow something from somebody and you lose it, should you buy them a new one?

If you borrow something and it breaks, should you pay for the repair?

If you borrow something and another person steals it, should you pay for a new one?

Does it depend on what it is? Think about these objects:

a piece of paper   a pencil   a sweater   a watch   a car

2 It's not fair!

2.1 Samantha's cassette

Listen to Rebecca and Samantha. Why is Samantha unhappy? Do you think the cassette is Steve's responsibility? Was it his fault?

REBECCA: What's wrong, Sam? You don't look very happy.

SAMANTHA: I'm not. It's not fair. Look at this.

REBECCA: What's that?

SAMANTHA: It's my favourite cassette. I lent it to Steve and this is what happened to it.

REBECCA: What! What did he do to it?

SAMANTHA: *He* didn't do anything. His sister's dog chewed it. It's completely destroyed!

REBECCA: So? What's the problem? Steve can buy you a new cassette.

SAMANTHA: That's what I think, but he says it's not his fault. He says he won't pay for it.

REBECCA: What! He *has* to pay for it.

SAMANTHA: Well, he won't pay for it. It's not fair.

REBECCA: Come on, let's go and talk to him.

What do you think Steve is going to say?

2.2 With Steve

Listen to Samantha, Rebecca and Steve.

What does Steve tell Samantha to do?
Why won't Mrs Wilson help Samantha, do you think?

REBECCA: Hi, Steve. Samantha has just told me about her cassette.

STEVE: Oh, yes. It's terrible isn't it. It's my sister's fault.

SAMANTHA: It was your responsibility, Steve.

STEVE: You have to talk to my sister about it.

SAMANTHA: I lent it to you, Steve, not to your sister.

REBECCA: That's right, Steve. You should buy Samantha a new cassette.

STEVE: I can't. I haven't got any money. Anyway, it's not my fault. I didn't destroy it. I'd put it away in my drawer and my sister took it out.

REBECCA: That's not the point, Steve. You have to buy a new cassette for Samantha. Then, you can get the money from your sister.

STEVE: Look, stay out of it, Rebecca. It's none of your business.

REBECCA: Yes, it is, Steve, Sam's my friend.

STEVE: Well, I've told you. I haven't got any money.

SAMANTHA: You can borrow some money, can't you?

STEVE: No.

REBECCA: Let's go and ask Mrs Wilson, Sam.

STEVE: Mrs Wilson! You'll be lucky after that business with her handbag.

SAMANTHA: Be quiet, Steve.

REBECCA: He's right, Samantha. Mrs Wilson won't help us.

SAMANTHA: Well, I know what I can do. I'm going to …

Is it Rebecca's 'business'? What should Samantha do next, do you think? Have you ever been in a situation like that?

2.3 Some ideas

Here are some things that Samantha can do next. Which ones might help? Which ones might make the situation worse? Why?

She can talk to another teacher.
She can talk to Steve's sister.
She can talk to the head teacher.
She can take something of Steve's.
She can talk to Steve's parents.
She can never speak to Steve again.

3 Inside the text

Look back through the dialogue in Exercise 2. Can you find these phrases? How do you say them in your language?

It's not fair.   What's the problem?   Stay out of it.
Let's go and talk to him.   It's not my fault.
It's none of your business.   You'll be lucky.

Add the phrases to your *Record of Language Use*.

4 Decide …

Work by yourself or in a small group. Choose an exercise.

4.1 What happened next?

Who did Samantha talk to next? Look at the list in Exercise 2.3 and prepare a conversation. Act out your conversation for the class.

4.2 What do you think?

Look back at the questions in Exercise 1. Write what you think about each question.

4.3 You decide!

Look at page 91 for ideas. You could:

– write a poem about an argument with a friend.
– write about something valuable that was broken.
– write a story about something that breaks.

Work by yourself. Answer the questions in the questionnaire.

Discuss your answers with other students in your class. How can you prepare for tests better?

Questionnaire
Preparing for tests

1 Do you prepare for tests?
- ❏ Always.
- ❏ Usually.
- ❏ Sometimes.
- ❏ Almost never.

Why?

2 Where do you usually prepare for tests?
- ❏ In a quiet place.
- ❏ In a noisy place.
- ❏ At a table.
- ❏ Lying on my bed.
- ❏ While I am watching TV.
- ❏ While I am eating.
- ❏ Alone.
- ❏ With a friend or friends.
- ❏ Somewhere else:

3 What kind of preparation works best for you?
- ❏ Learning by heart.
- ❏ Trying to understand a rule.
- ❏ Remembering some example sentences.
- ❏ Telling someone else about what I've learned.
- ❏ Making a lot of notes.
- ❏ Doing more exercises.
- ❏ Something else:

4 When do you prepare for a test?
- ❏ The night before, studying late into the night.
- ❏ Little by little a few days before.
- ❏ On the day the teacher tells us about the test.
- ❏ A few minutes before the test.
- ❏ Something other time:

By yourself, think about some tests that you have recently had. Make a list. What did you do to prepare for them? Were there any surprises in the tests? Were they easier or more difficult than you expected? Compare ideas with other students in your class.

AROUND THE THEME

1 What's on TV?

1.1 What would you watch?

Look at part of a TV guide. Which programmes would you watch? Which programmes would you definitely *not* watch? Why? Tell the class.

1.2 Which programme?

Which programmes are:

a about science?
b about the lives of women?
c about boys and girls?

d about sport?
e films?
f music?

2 Take a look at Theme F

Look at the pictures in the TV guide. Where can you find them in Units 16-18 and Optional Unit F?

What is each Unit about? Match each Unit to one of the descriptions (a–f) in Exercise 1.2.

TV1

6.00	**News and Weather.**
7.00	**100 Years of Working Women.** A report on women's work over the last century. Have things changed much for women?

Women at work, 1915

8.00	**Sports Night: Football Special.** The World Cup.
8.45	**The Alan Minton Show.** Comedy and music.
10.00	**News and Weather.**
10.45	**Media Report.** Tonight from the USA.

TV2

5.30	**Longton.** The continuing story of the pupils at Longton School.
6.00	**News.**
6.15	**Science Today.** Left or right? Fascinating images of the workings of our brains

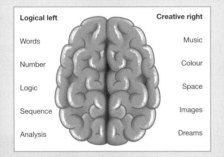

Logical left — Words, Number, Logic, Sequence, Analysis

Creative right — Music, Colour, Space, Images, Dreams

7.00	**Politics Today.**
7.30	**Film: The Silent City.** A science fiction film about a team of scientists who are looking for oil. Everything goes well until some strange things start happening and a powerful mirage appears in front of them. An excellent film with beautiful photography.
9.20	**News.**
9.45	**The Rock Programme.** More late night music from the world of rock.
10.30	**The Travel Programme.** Tonight – the mountains of Peru.

TV3

7.00	**The Mandy Green Report.** More and more girls go to university. Are they getting better jobs? Do they earn more money?
7.45	**High Life.** Another Australian series.
8.30	**The Sports Programme.** Results from all of today's sports events.
9.00	**Customer Report.** Tonight: presents for children. What are the best toys to give young children? What do children really like? Find out in Customer Report!

10.00	**Film: A Walk in the Sun.** A classic western.
11.30	**Late Night News.**

Stereotypes:
curriculum links
with Sociology
and Social
Studies; 'used to'

1 *Discussion*

2 *Reading*
WB Exs. 1, 2; IT A
and B

Inside the text
A *Comprehension*
B *Vocabulary*

16 Change
Topic and language

1 Changes

1.1 Changes where you live

How has your school, town or country changed in the last few years? Think for a few moments and note down your ideas.

> We used to have only a small library. Now we have a lot of books.
> Our town used to be very small. Now it is much bigger.

Tell the class your ideas.

1.2 People in your country

Think about the different people in your country. How have their lives changed in the last ten, twenty or thirty years?
Work with a partner and write some ideas under each heading.

Children's lives	The lives of old people
The lives of people in towns	The lives of people in the country

Write some sentences about your ideas and then tell the class.

2 Women's lives

2.1 True or false?

Read the following statements. Are they true (T) or false (F), do you think? Compare your answers with other students.

a There are more men than women in the world. ☐

b Women own 40% of the world's land. ☐

c About 50% of the world's labour force is female. ☐

d In most places, women earn the same salary as men. ☐

e Half of the top ten richest people in the world are women. ☐

f Boys usually do better than girls at school. ☐

2.2 Changes in women's lives

In many countries, the lives of women have changed a lot in the last hundred years. What do you think has caused this change?

Read about changes in women's lives. Check your answers to Exercise 2.1.

🔲 You can listen to the text on the cassette.

CHANGES IN WOMEN'S LIVES

There are many different reasons why women's lives have changed. Part of the reason is industrialisation. Many women moved away from rural areas where they used to work in agriculture, to the towns and cities.

Working in factories

During World War I (1914–18) and World War II (1939–45), many men went away to fight. This meant that more and more women had to work outside the home. For many women, this was the first time that they were independent and that they had their own money. They were not wealthy, but many women were not so poor as they used to be.

Voting in elections

In many countries, women also started to fight for the right to vote in elections and to make political decisions.

Education for women

Other important changes affected the lives of many women. First, in many countries more girls started to go to school. In the past, people used to send only their sons to school, not their daughters. Many people thought that education was too expensive to 'waste' on girls.

LIFE TODAY: SOME FACTS AND FIGURES

*Life for many women **has** changed, but in some parts of the world it is still the same as it used to be 100 years ago.*

◆ Over 50% of the world's population is female but women own less than 10% of the world's land.
◆ On average, women earn 65% of the salary of men.
◆ There are no women in the list of the world's 100 richest people.

◆ More than three times more women than men cannot read or write.
◆ In school, girls generally do better than boys but boys generally get better jobs when they leave school.
◆ In some countries, only 10% of the labour force is female.

Inside the text

A Linking ideas

Find these phrases and sentences in the text. What do the words *like this* refer to?

1 ... very different from life in the time of *their* grandmothers.
2 ... *they* used to work in agriculture.
3 ... *they* had their own money.
4 ... *their* sons to school, not *their* daughters.
5 ... *it* is still the same as *it* used to be.
6 ... when *they* leave school.

B Opposites

Look at the words in Box 1. Can you find the opposite word in Box 2?

Box 1	Box 2
wealthy	traditional
modern	industry
son	rural
different	the same
urban	daughter
agriculture	poor

3 'used to'
WB Ex. 3

4 Listening
5 Language
Record

3 Language focus 'used to'

3.1 Past, present or future?

Look at these sentences. Are they talking about the past, the present or the future? How do you say them in your language?

> People used to send only their sons to school.
> Many women used to work in agriculture.

What is the difference in meaning between each sentence in these pairs?

> He used to come to our school.
> He came to our school yesterday.
>
> She used to play the guitar.
> She played the guitar last night.
>
> We didn't use to play football at primary school.
> We didn't play football yesterday.

Can you find some more examples with 'used to' in the text in Exercise 2?

3.2 How to use 'used to'

You can use 'used to' to talk about things that happened regularly in the past and that don't happen now.

> I used to go to bed at 8 o'clock. Now I go to bed at 10 o'clock.
> They used to live in a house. Now they live in a flat.
> She used to go to Central Primary School. Now she comes to our school.

You can use 'used to' for all persons.

I You He/She/It We You They	used to live in a house. used to go to bed at 8 o'clock. used to go to Central Primary School.

You can make questions with 'did' and negatives with 'didn't'.

> What school did you use to go to?
> I didn't use to walk to school. Now I walk to school every day.

You can also say:

> I never used to walk to school.

3.3 PRACTICE When you were 11 …

Interview your neighbour. Ask him/her about when he/she was younger.

Which school did you use to go to?

What games did you use to play?

What did you use to like to eat or drink?

What did you use to do at weekends?

What did you use to hate?

What did you use to watch on TV?

3.4 What are the differences?

Look at the pictures of London. How has London changed? Write about the pictures. For example:

One hundred years ago, people used to use horses a lot. Today, everybody travels by car. One hundred years ago, women used to wear long dresses. Today, they wear trousers and shorter dresses.

4 Women's lives, a long time ago

Dr Hollett is talking about the lives of women 5,000 years ago. Can you complete the notes?

There were two types of societies: _____ and _____ .

In military societies, women had a _____ status.

In agricultural societies, women had a _____ status.

In Egypt, women _____

In Crete, women _____

Compare your notes with other students.

Present day

100 years ago

5 Your Language Record

5.1 Your Grammar Record

Make notes about 'used to' in your *Grammar Record*. Make notes about how to form it and how to use it. Look at Exercise 3 and the Language summaries in your Workbook for ideas.

5.2 Your Record of Language Use

Look back at Unit 16. Are there more words and phrases you want to add to your *Record of Language Use*? Check your record with this list.

Nouns labour force   salary   'top ten' part ('an active part') industrialisation   agriculture   industry   World War   election politician   male   female   catalogue   gun   construction equipment

Verbs used to   earn   take place   vote   provide record (on a cassette)   expect   encourage   notice

Adjectives active   rural   urban   independent   wealthy poor   dirty   messy   loud   passive   nice   dark   bright logical   beautiful   handsome   cruel   ugly   lonely

Adverbs more than   less than   generally   on average

Time to spare?

Choose one of these exercises.

1 Look at the *Help yourself list* on page 91. Make an exercise about this Unit.

2 Write about the differences between your last school and your school now like this:

At my last school I used to finish lessons at 2 o'clock but now I finish at 4 o'clock.

3 What other differences do you think there are for boys and girls? Write about one of these topics.

sports activities   playing musical instruments activities with friends

17 FOCUS ON
Boys and girls

1 *Fluency*
2 *Writing*
3 *You decide!*

1 Focus on boys and girls

1.1 What do you think?

Before you read the texts, discuss these questions with your class.

a What colours do boys and girls wear? Does this change when they get older?

b Do adults talk to boys and girls in the same way?

c In traditional stories, what are the girls like? What are the boys like?

d What types of toys do people give to young boys? What types of toys do they give to young girls?

1.2 Search!

Look at the texts. Which text is about each of the questions in Exercise 1.1?
Where do you expect to find the following phrases?

'they get more active toys'
'wear pink and boys wear'
'the main girl character is usually "lovely"'
'What a nice dress!'

Read the texts to check your answers.
Do you think the same things are true in your country?

1.3 What's the word?

Part of the reason why girls and boys *are* different is that people *think* about boys and girls in different ways. Read through the texts again. What adjectives describe boys? What adjectives describe girls? Make two lists.

Boys   Girls

Compare your lists with your partner.

2 Decide ...

Choose a or b.

a Write an advertisement for a toy or a game that you think would be good for boys *and* girls of your age. Draw a picture and write about it. Say *why* it is good for boys *and* girls.

b Decide what *you* want to do and ask your teacher. You could:

– write a poem about being a girl or a boy.
– write about the differences between boys and girls.
– write about the toys that you think people should give to young children.

Look at the *Help yourself list* on page 91 for ideas.

Clothes and colour

Girls and boys often wear different colours. If you look in clothes shops and catalogues, you can often see that, when children are small, the girls wear pink and the boys wear blue.

When the boys are a few years older, the clothes are much darker. They wear brown, black, grey or dark blue. When girls get older they often wear brighter colours – yellow, purple, bright green. We don't often see boys who are wearing yellow or pink when they are 13 or 14 years old.

Language differences

Many adults expect boys to get dirty, to be messy or to be loud when they play. They say things like 'Boys will be boys' or 'Boys are like that'. People often encourage boys to be strong. They say things like 'Be a big man', 'Don't be a baby!' 'What a big, strong boy!'

Many adults expect girls to be quieter and more passive than boys. They often talk about a girl's clothes or how pretty she is. They say things like 'She's as pretty as a picture', 'She's a big help at home' or 'What a nice dress!'

Toys for boys and toys for girls

There are many differences in 'boys' toys and 'girls' toys. Boys often have more freedom to run around and they get more active toys than girls – guns, train sets, sports equipment, cars and electronic games were the most popular toys for young boys.

There are also many construction toys for boys. We think that toy manufacturers think boys are more logical than girls.

Toys for girls are much quieter and more passive. Young girls often get things like dolls, dresses, jewellery, pictures to colour and toy kitchen tools.

Stories for young children

In many traditional stories for very young children, the main girl character is usually 'lovely' or 'beautiful' and is waiting for the 'handsome' prince. The other girls in the stories are often cruel or ugly. The main girl character never seems to have any friends. She seems very lonely.

The main boy character usually does all the exciting things – riding horses or travelling or chopping down trees. A lot of films also have these kinds of characters and stories in them.

18 Revision

1 How well do you know it?

How well do you think you know the English you learnt in units 16–17? Put a tick (√) in the table.

Now choose some sections to revise and practise.

	very well	OK	a little
Vocabulary			
Gerunds and prepositions			
Imperatives			
Used to			
Relative clauses			

2 The words you met

Can you write the correct words in the puzzle?

1 The person who decides exactly what will happen in each scene of a film. (d.....................)

2 You see a film on a television or cinema s...................... .

3 This is a c...................... .

4 The casting director c........................... all the actors and actresses.

5 The person who cuts and checks the film. (e.........................)

6 A lot of people together. (c..........................)

7 The person who creates the story for a film. (w.........................)

8 If something is t........................, you can see through it.

9 A film about cowboys is called a w...................... .

10 You take photographs with a c...................... .

11 An actor is a man. An a........................... is a woman.

3 The stunt actors

Read about stunt actors. Put a circle around the preposition and then complete the text with a gerund.

Dangerous work for stunt actors

Most 'film stars' do not want to do dangerous things. They are afraid (of)
___hurting___ (hurt) themselves! Instead, the director employs 'stunt' actors who
are expert at [1] _____ (do) difficult and dangerous acts. For example, if the
'star' has to fall from a horse, a stunt actor who specialises in [2] _____ (work)
with horses does it instead. The stunt actor has the job of [3] _____ (fall)
from the horse without [4] _____ (injure) himself. By
[5] _____ (film) the face of the 'star' and the body of the
stunt actor, the director tricks us into [6] _____ (think)
that the 'star' is really doing it.

4 I'm interested in ...

Can you write the correct form of the verb in each gap?

a

I'm very interested in
_____. (learn) English.

b

He's very lazy, so instead of _____
(walk) to school, he comes by bus.

c

She's good at _____
(ride) a horse.

d

Are you afraid of _____ (fly)?

e

He's very happy about _____
(pass) his examination.

f

They bend metal by
_____ (make) it very hot.

5 How to watch a video

How can you watch a film on video?
Put the instructions in the correct order.

- ☐ **a** When you have done that, you put the video into the video machine.
- ☐ **b** Next, you switch the television and the video machine on.
- ☐ **c** First, you take the video out of the box.
- ☐ **d** Finally, you press the 'Play' button and watch the film.
- ☐ **e** Then you set the television to the correct channel.

6 Everything used to be so different!

6.1 The school news

Look at the pictures. Write about the changes in the school.

The science laboratory

The library

School News

Last week Mr Burnside, who used to come to Central School, sent us these old photos. Everything is so different now! Look how the school has changed. The playground used to have nothing in it. Now we've got equipment to play on!
The library

The playground

The school hall

6.2 Changes in your town or school

Write five sentences to describe changes in your school or town. For example:

Our school used to be very small but now there are 2,000 students here.

6.3 How do you use 'used to'?

Are these sentences true or false? Write 'T' or 'F'.

1 'Used to' is the same for all persons (I, you, he, we, etc.). ☐

2 After 'used to' you use the infinitive. ☐

3 We use 'used to' to talk about something which happened regularly in the past. ☐

4 The negative of 'used to' is 'didn't use to'. ☐

5 We often use 'used to' when we talk about something which has changed. ☐

Find some examples in Unit 16 and in your language summaries to prove your answers. Compare with other students in the class.

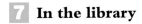 **In the library**

Look at the picture. Can you answer questions 1–10? Write your answers.

Who has got a blue coat? *The woman who is writing a letter.*

1 Who is talking on the telephone?
2 Who has got a bicycle helmet?
3 What is the woman looking for?
4 Who is listening to music?
5 Who has got two shopping bags?
6 Who is sleeping?
7 Which light is on?
8 Who has got a red T-shirt?
9 Which window is open?
10 Which telephone is ringing?

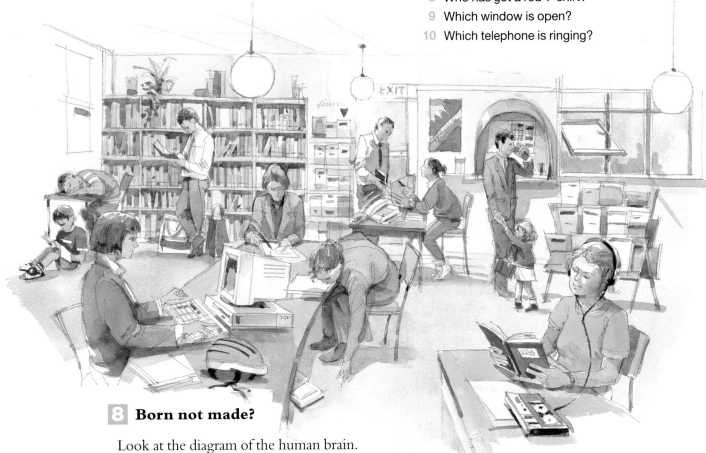

8 **Born not made?**

Look at the diagram of the human brain. Read about the brain and complete the gaps in the text with the relative clauses a–f.

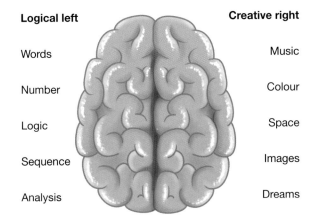

Logical left	Creative right
Words	Music
Number	Colour
Logic	Space
Sequence	Images
Analysis	Dreams

Some scientists, *who have studied babies' brains*, say they have found differences between boys and girls. They say the brain, ..., develops differently in boys and girls. They say the left side of the brain, ..., develops earlier in girls. The right side of the brain, ..., develops earlier in boys. Other scientists, ..., say that children learn these differences from other people. They say that adults, ..., 'teach' children to be different.

a ... which is responsible for music and colour ...
b ... who have studied babies' brains ...
c ... which has two hemispheres or parts ...

d ... who watch children's development ...
e ... which is responsible for number and logic ...
f ... who talk to boys and girls in different ways ...

1 **Work by yourself. Answer the questions in the first part of the questionnaire.**

Discuss your answers with other students in your class. How can you get extra practice?

Questionnaire
Getting extra practice

1 **Do you get extra English language practice outside the classroom?**
☐ Always. Usually.
☐ Sometimes.
☐ Almost never.
Why?

2 **Where do you usually get extra practice?**
☐ In a library.
☐ At home.
☐ In a language laboratory.
☐ Using a computer.
☐ Having extra language lessons.
☐ Another place:

3 **If you have a chance to have extra language practice what would you like to do?**
☐ Do more grammar exercises.
☐ Read magazines in English.
☐ Have a penfriend.
☐ Work on a project.
☐ Watch films in English.
☐ Use a computer.
☐ Travel to another country.
☐ Talk to other people in English.
☐ Something else:

4 **Would you like extra practice in**
☐ grammar?
☐ vocabulary?
☐ writing?
☐ reading?
☐ listening?
☐ speaking?
☐ something else?

5 **Do you think getting extra practice is useful? Why/why not?**

6 **Do you think you get enough extra practice? How much is a 'good' amount?**

2 Suggestion box

You are nearly at the end of the book. Have you got any suggestions or comments about the book?

2.1 Your suggestions

Work alone. Look back through the Student's Book and Workbook. Focus on one aspect of the book. For example, the pictures, the dialogues, the reading texts or the *Out and about* Units.

Can you make any comments and suggestions about this aspect? Write each suggestion on a separate piece of paper and put it in the box.

2.2 Do you agree?

Take some papers from the box and read them out to the class. Do other people in the class agree?

2.3 Tell the authors!

Write a letter, fax or e-mail to us. You can tell us about the comments in your *Suggestion box*, or give us your own suggestions or tell us what you would like to see in your English books.

Send your letter to:

AIR MAIL

Andrew Littlejohn and Diana Hicks,
c/o Cambridge University Press,
The Edinburgh Building,
Shaftesbury Road,
Cambridge CB2 2RU,
England.

Or send a fax to:
++ 44 1223 325984
Or send an e-mail message to:
aldh@cup.cam.ac.uk

Many thanks!

A

OPTIONAL UNIT
Britain is ~~is~~ an Island
Culture matters

1 Britain was an island

A long time ago, Britain was joined to France.
Then, about 8,000 years ago, the level of the
sea rose and Britain became an island.
The result was the Channel.

There are many different ways to cross
the Channel. You can cross:

by plane   by ferry   by hydrofoil
by catamaran   by hovercraft

Now, there is another way: by tunnel. Britain is not an island any more.

Have you been on a plane, ferry, catamaran, hydrofoil, hovercraft,
or through a long tunnel? Where did you go?

2 Through the tunnel!

Today, you can travel by train direct from London to Paris. The journey
is fast and comfortable. You can also take your car with you on one of the
super-fast trains, made especially for the tunnel.

🔊 Listen to the train announcement.
Can you answer these questions?

How long does the trip from London to Paris take?
How fast does the train go?
How long is the train in the tunnel?
How far under the sea is the tunnel?

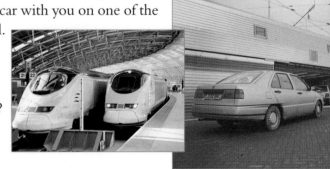

3 One of the Wonders of the World

Look at the information about the Channel Tunnel. Find answers to these questions.

a How many train tunnels are there?

b Is the tunnel *in* the sea or *under* the sea?

c How long did it take to build it?

d Where are the drills now?

●HOW DID THEY DO IT? ●

Three tunnels, not one

We talk about 'the Channel Tunnel' but, in fact, there are three tunnels, not one. There are two tunnels for trains and one service tunnel.

130 metres depth

sea

lighting

train tracks

Eurostar train

train tunnel (×2)

service tunnel for repairs and emergencies

SOME FACTS ABOUT THE TUNNEL

Cost: £10,000,000,000 ($15,000,000,000)

Size: 50 km long (total)

130 m under the sea

Maximum speed of trains in the tunnel:

130 km per hour for car trains

160 km per hour for passenger trains

Journey time in the tunnel: 21 minutes

Passengers in each train: 800

MAKING THE TUNNEL

The Channel Tunnel is one of the most incredible pieces of engineering. It opened in 1994 after six years of work. To build the tunnels, they used giant drills from both France and England. These special drills moved slowly underground and put up the walls of the tunnels and put down the train tracks at the same time. The French engineers took their drill out when the work was finished. The English engineers left their drill inside the tunnel. It was too expensive to take it out.

4 A good thing or a bad thing?

🔲 Not everyone in Britain is happy about the Channel Tunnel. Read what some people say about the tunnel. Do they think it is a good [G] or a bad [B] thing?

a
Millions of rats will run down the tunnel and bring diseases that we don't have here. ☐

b
This tunnel is fantastic. It means that we can now get to France much quicker. It is going to be excellent for business. ☐

c
Why do we want a tunnel? The tunnel is going to change our traditional British way of life. We are not an island any more. ☐

d
The tunnel saves me lots of time and I can do my work on the train. Before, it took hours and hours by plane or boat. ☐

e
I think it's great. I hate travelling by sea. I always feel sick. Now, with the tunnel, I can travel by train. ☐

5 Across cultures

How can you get from your country to the next country?

What do you think? Do you think it is a good idea to make it easier to travel from one country to another?

Revision of Units 4
and 5
Optional Unit B:
Extra practice

1 *Self
assessment*
2 *Vocabulary*
3 *Zero
conditional*
4 *Modals*
5 *Past
continuous*

B OPTIONAL UNIT
Revision

1 How well do you know it?

How well do you think you know the English you learnt in Theme B?
Put a tick (✔) in the table.
Now choose some sections to revise and practise.

	very well	*OK*	*a little*
Vocabulary			
Zero conditional			
Modals			
Past continuous			

2 The words you met

Can you write the correct words in the puzzle?

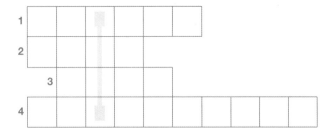

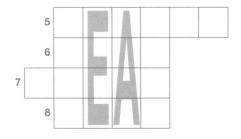

1 In 1642, there were more than 500 aboriginal
t................................. in Australia.

2 The *Marie Celeste* was a s.................................. .

3 Franklin took 8,000 t................................. of food
with him.

4 He also took many s.................................
instruments.

5 Many expeditions went to s.................................
for him.

6 Franklin and his men died of l.................................
poisoning.

7 Aborigines hunt with a s................................. .

8 Australia exports a lot of m................................. .

3 'If' and 'when'

Can you complete these sentences
with your own words?

1 If you watch too much television, …
2 If you eat too many sweets, …
3 If you eat too much bread, …
4 If you play with fire, …
5 When summer comes, …
6 When school starts, …
7 When the night comes, …
8 When the morning comes, …

4 You shouldn't do that!

Write 'should', 'might', 'need to', 'needn't', 'must', or
'mustn't' in each sentence.

1 You .... go to school when you are a child.
2 We .... go to school on Sundays.
3 It .... rain tomorrow.
4 You .... buy a ticket when you go on a bus.
5 You .... eat a lot of fruit.
6 You .... look before you
cross the road.
7 You .... sit too near to
the television.
8 You .... do homework
when you're an adult.
9 You ....
write on the wall.

5 A story from Malta

Can you put the correct form of the verb in the spaces?
(Use the Past continuous and Past simple. Look on page 90
for irregular verbs.)

Mystery in Malta

Many years ago in Malta, a young woman [1] *was driving*
(drive) her car near a place called Dingli Cliffs. She
[2] .... (go) home after a long day at work. Suddenly,
she [3] .... (see) a man in the road in front of her. He
[4] .... (wave) his arms in the air. He [5] ....
(wear) a long black coat and he had a beard. The woman
[6] .... (stop) the car and she [7] .... (ask) the
man what he wanted. The man said nothing. He just pointed
towards the cliffs.

The woman [8] .... (get out) and
she [9] .... (look) over the cliffs. Down
below, near the sea she could see a blue car. It
was upside down and it [10] ....
(burn). 'Oh, no!' the woman shouted, 'We must
call the ambulance!'

She turned round to tell the man but he
wasn't there. She looked down the cliffs again ...
and the car wasn't there either! The woman was
very frightened. She [11] .... (jump)
back into her car and [12] .... (drive)
into the city.

In the city, she [13] .... (go) straight
to the police station.

'What was the man wearing?' asked the
policeman.

'He [14] .... (wear) a long black
coat,' said the woman.

'Did the man have a beard?' asked the
policeman.

'Yes,' said the woman.

'What colour was the car?' asked the
policeman.

'Blue,' said the woman.

'Was the car burning?'

'Yes,' said the woman.

'That,' said the policeman, 'is the Ghost of
Dingli Cliffs. That accident [15] ....
(happen) 25 years ago. Every year on this day,
the man appears again to tell people what
happened to him.'

Modals – 'could',
'would'; prepositions
of place;

1 *Listening and reading*

2 *'could': making a request; speaking*
WB Extra practice

3 *'would': making an offer*

C OPTIONAL UNIT
Requests and offers
Fluency

1 On the road

🔊 Ken is a lorry driver in England. He takes containers to and from airports, ferries, railway stations and factories. Listen. Ken's boss is planning trips for next week.

Listen to their conversation. First, draw a line on the map to show where Ken has to go.

Listen again and complete Ken's worksheet.

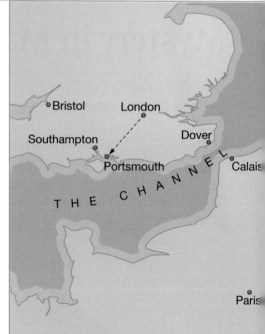

2 'Could you ...?'

2.1 Making a request

Ken's boss asked him to go to different places like this:

> Could you pick up some washing machines?

> Could you collect some pencils in Bristol?

> Could you drive back to London?

How do you say the same things in your language?

	Morning	Afternoon
Mon	Portsmouth	
Tues		
Wed		
Thurs		
Fri		

2.2 Who says what?

Match the sentences to the pictures.

1 (Could you open your suitcase, please?)

3 (Could you finish this exercise for Friday, please?)

5 (Could you turn the music down, please?)

2 (Could you answer the phone, Tim?)

4 (Could you lend me your new cassette tonight?)

6 (Could you tell me where Smith's supermarket is, please?)

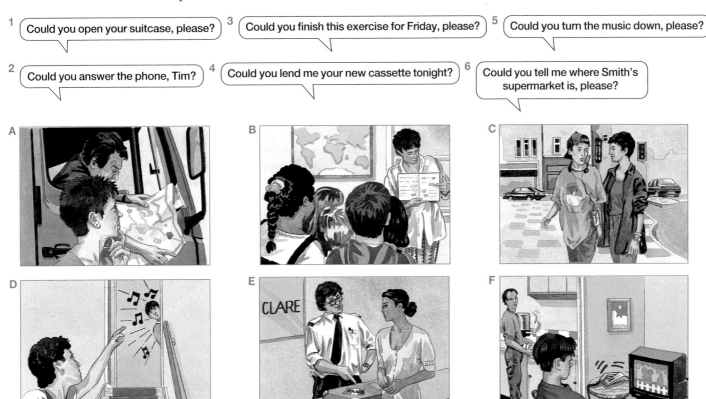

Check your answers with your partner. What can the people in the pictures answer?

You can listen to the dialogues on the cassette.

2.3 Play a game! What do you want?

Work in a small group (or with the whole class). Mime a request. The other students have to guess what you are asking. For example:

The person who guesses correctly has the next turn. You can use these verbs:

lend   show   give   open   help   bring   carry   write   put

3 'Would you like ...?'

Ken's boss asks him: (Would you like to have a rest on Friday?)

Here are some more examples

(Would you like a sandwich?)

(No, thanks. I'm not hungry.)

(Would you like to go to the cinema?)

(Yes, please. I love watching films!)

MULTI SCREEN
ADMIT 1
TIME : 14:30

How do you say these sentences in your language?

Asking the way

1 *Brainstorming*
2 *Speaking*
3 *Directions*
4 *Listening*
5 *Practice*

WB Optional Unit
D: Fluency practice

OPTIONAL UNIT
Asking the way
Fluency

1 Can you tell me where it is?

1.1 Going shoppping

Helen and Will are on holiday. They ask some people the way to a supermarket. What do you think they say?

Brainstorm your ideas with the class.

1.2 Let's ask someone

Listen to Helen and Will. Are you right?

2 Asking the way

Work in pairs. Look at the map. Ask each other where each place is.

– Excuse me. Do you know where's the post office is?
– yes, it's in Green Street, next to the newsagent's.

Excuse me. Could you tell me where...is?
Excuse me. Where can I find .....

next to   in front of   behind   on the left of
on the right of

Act out a conversation for the class.

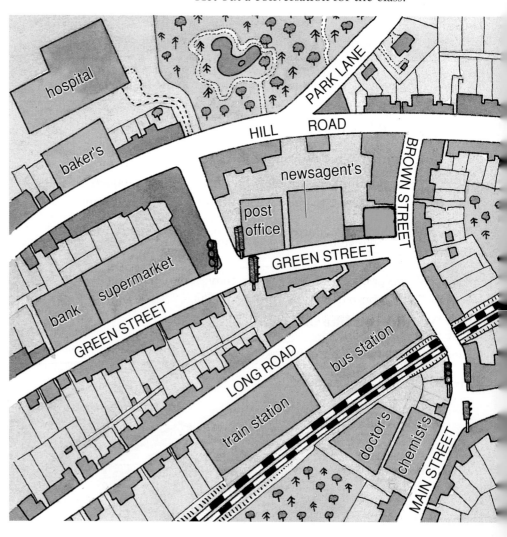

3 Left or right?

Can you match the phrase to the correct picture?

a Turn left   b Turn right   c Go straight on
d Take the second turning on the left
e Take the third turning on the right
f It's on the corner
g Turn left at the traffic lights.

4 Will, Helen and the Concert Hall

Will and Helen are still looking for the concert hall. Listen to the conversations. Look at the map. What street is the information office in?

HELEN: We're not going to find the concert hall. Lets forget it.

WILL: Come on, Helen! I told you. We have to ask someone. I can ask in the chemists.

WOMAN: Yes, dear?

WILL: Could you tell me where the concert hall is?

WOMAN: The concert hall? There isn't a concert hall in this town.

WILL: Oh no! We saw a poster for a concert tomorrow.

WOMAN: Oh, I see. The concert hall is in Bington, the next town but you can tickets here in the tourist information office.

WILL: Oh, good! That's what we were looking for.

WOMAN: OK, well it's not far but it's a bit complicated. You go out here and turn left. Then you turn left again at the traffic lights. Go straight on and take the second turning on the left. The tourist information is on the right, on the corner.

WILL: Oh dear! I go left and left again. Then it's the second turning on the left and the office is on the right. On a corner.

WOMAN: That's right.

WILL: Oh thank you. I think I can remember. Bye.

WOMAN: Bye.

HELEN: Well, did you find out?

WILL: The concert hall is in the next town! But we can buy tickets in the tourist information office, here.

HELEN: Where's that?

WILL: Well, we go left and then left again. or is it right? No, it's left and then left and then right. Or is it straight on? Oh, no! I can't remember!

5 Now you try it

Look at the map. You are at the bus station. Choose two places and write directions to get there. Don't say which place it is!

Read your directions to your neighbour. He/She has to guess which place it is.

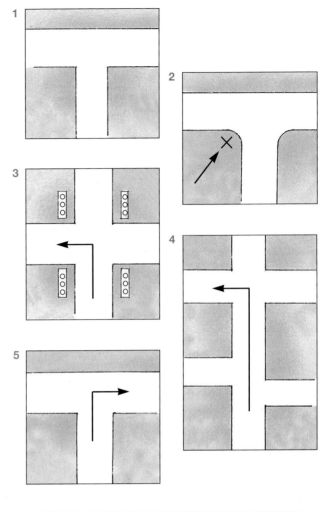

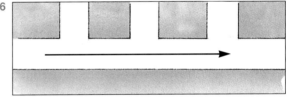

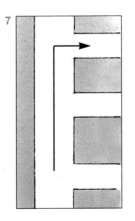

Native Americans
in the United
States
WB Optional
Unit E: Fluency
practice

1 *Discussion*

2 *Reading*

3 *Listening*

4 *Research and
writing*

OPTIONAL UNIT
Native Americans in the USA
Culture matters

1 Cowboys and Indians?

Have you seen any 'cowboys and Indians' films?
Many of the ideas that we have about Native
Americans in the United States of America
come from films about 'cowboys and Indians'.
Note down your answers to these questions:

Why do you think people call them 'Indians'?
Where in North America did they live?
How did they live? What did they eat?
Why did they fight white people?
Where do they live today? How do they live?
How many Native Americans are there?

Discuss your ideas with other students in your
class.

2 The Native Americans

2.1 Are you right?

Many of the stories about American 'Indians'
in the films are completely wrong. Read about
the history of the Native Americans. Which
questions from Exercise 1 can you answer now?
Which questions can't you answer?

2.2 What do you think?

Do you think what happened to the Native
Americans is fair? What do you think should
happen today?

3 The Native Americans today

3.1 On the reservations

David Mulgee is a Native American who
now works at the University of California. He
is talking to Lyndsey Ban about the Native
Americans today. Listen. Can you answer the
last three questions in Exercise 1?

3.2 Listen again

Copy this list and listen to the
conversation again. Can you complete the
information?

Number of Native Americans today:
Number of reservations:
Most reservations have their own:
Industries on the reservations:
Problems on the reservations:

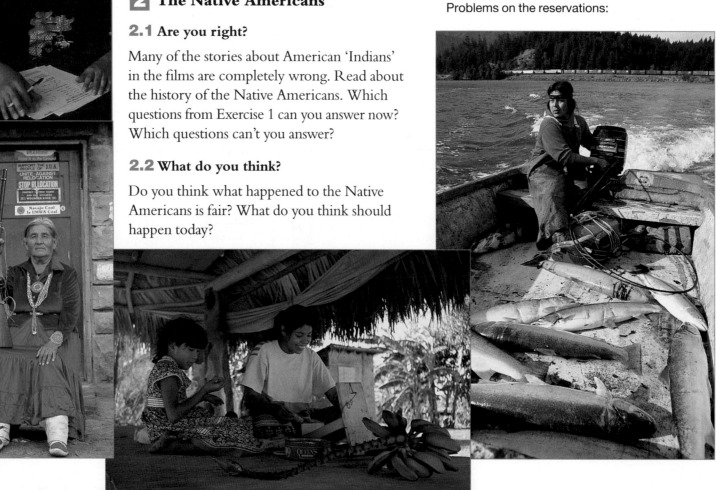

THE NATIVE AMERICANS

BEFORE COLUMBUS

When Columbus arrived in the Caribbean in 1492, he thought he had landed in the East Indies in Asia, so he called the people there 'Indians'. In fact, they were Native Americans, who had arrived in the Americas over 40,000 years before him.

At that time, Native Americans lived all over North America. Many of them lived in small groups of about 20–50 people. Most of them were very peaceful people, who lived by hunting and collecting food. Other Native Americans lived in small villages where they had farms. The Native Americans were the first people to cultivate many of the plants that we now eat: potatoes, beans, maize, tomatoes, pineapples, cacao and many more. There were thousands of different languages and tribes, each with its own culture.

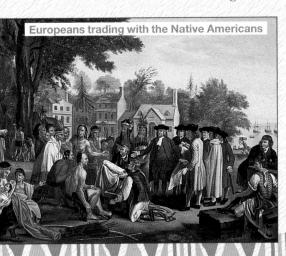
Europeans trading with the Native Americans

THE ARRIVAL OF THE EUROPEANS

When the Europeans arrived, they tried to take land away from the Native Americans and there were many wars. Millions of Native Americans also died from the diseases that the Europeans brought with them. As the Europeans took control over the eastern part of North America, the Native Americans had to move to the west in order to survive.

After the United States became independent, white Americans moved

Chief Sitting Bull, 1885

Wounded Knee, 1890

further west into the lands where Native Americans lived, and there were many battles – as we can see in the 'cowboys and Indians' films. Then, starting in 1830, the US Government forced the Native Americans to move even further west into 'reservations'. The Native Americans fought against this, and for many years there were wars against the white Americans, ending with the massacre of Sioux men, women and children at Wounded Knee in 1890.

---

4 Decide ... Across cultures

Choose a or b.

a Native inhabitants of your country

Who were the original inhabitants of your country? Are there descendants of those people alive today? Find out about where they live, and what they do today. Collect some pictures and write about them.

b From America to your country

Here is a list of many things that Native Americans first farmed. Can you find out when they first arrived in your country and who brought them there?

potatoes beans maize tomatoes
pineapples cacao chilli peppers cashews
squashes artichokes sweet potatoes
turkeys tobacco rubber

American and
British English

WB Optional Unit F
Help yourself with …

1 *Discussion*

2 *Listening*

3 *Reading*

4 *Research*

OPTIONAL UNIT
American English
Culture matters

1 Your language

Are there big differences in the way people speak your language? Are there some words that are only used in certain places? What differences in pronunciation are there?

2 English across the Atlantic

2.1 Words you know

Do you know any words from American English? Can you tell the difference between British and American English? How do British and American English sound different?

2.2 British or American?

Listen to six people speaking. Are they British or American, do you think? Write 'BE' or 'AE' for each one.

1   2   3   4   5   6

Compare your answers with other students.

3 Some differences

3.1 Some confusions

Read about some differences between British and American English. Look at the pictures and answer these questions.

Why is it all right to walk on the pavement in Britain, but not a good idea in the USA?

If you asked for chips in an American restaurant, why would the waiter be surprised?

Why would people in Britain be surprised if you asked for gas for your car?

3.2 Where are they from?

Read these sentences. Where does each person come from – Britain or America?

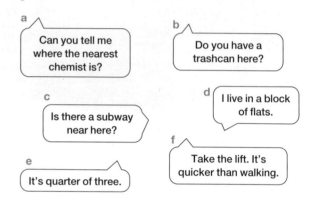

a Can you tell me where the nearest chemist is?

b Do you have a trashcan here?

c Is there a subway near here?

d I live in a block of flats.

e It's quarter of three.

f Take the lift. It's quicker than walking.

4 Decide …
Investigate British and American English

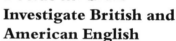

Choose **a** or **b**.

a American English

Find an American newspaper or magazine and choose a paragraph of text. Are there any examples of American words, grammar or spelling?

b English in your language

Are there many English words in your language? Make a list. Do they come from Britain or America, do you think?

ENGLISH ACROSS THE ATLANTIC

When the British landed in North America in 1620, they took their language with them. Since then, British English (BE) and American English (AE) have developed separately, and there are now some differences between them. The differences are quite small, however, and speakers of American and British English usually have no problems understanding each other.

Vocabulary

Here are some vocabulary differences.

UK English

1 jam
  crisps
  chips
  biscuits
2 Give Way
3 underground
4 block of flats
5 lift
6 flyover
7 WC/toilet
8 chemist
9 lorry
10 dustbin
11 pavement
12 petrol station
13 tarmac
14 boot
15 bonnet
16 car
17 postbox
18 pushchair

USA English

1 jelly
  chips
  French fries
  cookies
2 Yield
3 subway
4 apartment building
5 elevator
6 overpass
7 restrooms
8 drugstore
9 truck
10 trashcan
11 sidewalk
12 gas station
13 pavement
14 trunk
15 hood
16 auto
17 mailbox
18 stroller

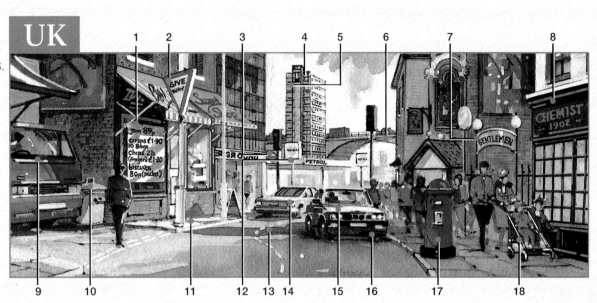

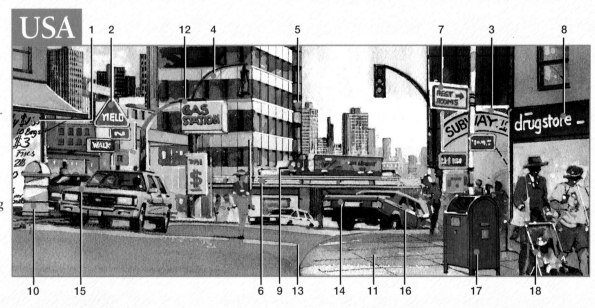

Spelling

American English uses '-or', where British English uses '-our'.
 AE: color   neighbor
 BE: colour   neighbour
American English uses '-er', where British English uses '-re'.
 AE: center   theater
 BE: centre   theatre

Grammar

American and British English sometimes use different prepositions.
 AE: It's twenty of six. It's five after nine.
 BE: It's twenty to six. It's five past nine.
American English doesn't use the Present perfect as much as British English.
 AE: I think I broke my leg.
 BE: I think I've broken my leg.

Pronunciation

'r' is often not pronounced in British English. It is always pronounced in American English.
 AE: car /kɑːr/ hard /hɑːrd/
 BE: car /kɑː/ hard /hɑːd/
'a' is usually short in American English but often long in British English.
 AE: ask /æsk/ banana /bə'nænə/
 BE: ask /ɑːsk/ banana /bə'nɑːnə/

Irregular verbs

Infinitive	Past simple	Past participle	Infinitive	Past simple	Past participle	Infinitive	Past simple	Past participle
be	was, were	been	hang	hung	hung	set	set	set
become	became	become	have	had	had	shake	shook	shaken
begin	began	begun	hear	heard	heard	shine	shone	shone
bite	bit	bitten	hide	hid	hidden	shoot	shot	shot
blow	blew	blown	hit	hit	hit	show	showed	shown
break	broke	broken	hold	held	held			showed
bring	brought	brought	hurt	hurt	hurt	shut	shut	shut
build	built	built				sing	sang	sung
buy	bought	bought	keep	kept	kept	sink	sank	sunk
			know	knew	known	sit	sat	sat
can	could	—				sleep	slept	slept
catch	caught	caught	lay	laid	laid	slide	slid	slid
choose	chose	chosen	lead	led	led	speak	spoke	spoken
come	came	come	lean	leant	leant	spell	spelt	spelt
cost	cost	cost	leave	left	left		spelled	spelled
cut	cut	cut	lend	lent	lent	spend	spent	spent
			let	let	let	spread	spread	spread
dig	dug	dug	lie	lay	lain	stand	stood	stood
do	did	done	light	lit	lit	steal	stole	stolen
draw	drew	drawn		lighted	lighted	stick	stuck	stuck
drink	drank	drunk	lose	lost	lost	sting	stung	stung
drive	drove	driven				swim	swam	swum
			make	made	made	swing	swung	swung
eat	ate	eaten	mean	meant	meant			
			meet	met	met	take	took	taken
fall	fell	fallen				teach	taught	taught
feed	fed	fed	pay	paid	paid	tell	told	told
feel	felt	felt	put	put	put	think	thought	thought
fight	fought	fought				throw	threw	thrown
find	found	found	read	read	read			
fly	flew	flown	ride	rode	ridden	understand	understood	understood
forget	forgot	forgotten	ring	rang	rung			
forgive	forgave	forgiven	rise	rose	risen			
freeze	froze	frozen	run	ran	run	wake	woke	woken
						wear	wore	worn
get	got	got	say	said	said	win	won	won
give	gave	given	see	saw	seen	wind	wound	wound
go	went	gone	sell	sold	sold	write	wrote	written
grow	grew	grown	send	sent	sent			

Help yourself list

Here are some ideas to give you more practice in English. You can work by yourself or with other students.

If you make an exercise for other students, remember to put the answers and your name on the back of the paper.

Closed exercises

These exercises have only one correct answer.

Idea 1 **What's the question?**

Write some questions and answers. Copy the answers.
Leave space for the questions.

1 Hello. How are you?
  I'm fine, thanks.
2 Where are you going?
  I'm going to the shops.
3 What are you going to buy?
  A new pair of shoes.

What's the question?

1 ....?
  I'm fine, thanks.
2 ....?
  I'm going to the shops.
3 ....?
  A new pair of shoes.

Idea 2 **Fill in the missing words.**

Choose a paragraph and take out some words.

The first people in America probably arrived there about 40,000 years ago. Because of the ice, the sea level was lower then and there was dry land between Asia and North America. People crossed over the land and travelled south into North and South America.

Fill in the missing words.

The first people in America probably .... there about 40,000 years .... Because of the ice, the sea level was .... then and there was dry .... between Asia and North America. People .... over the land and travelled south into North .... South America.

Idea 3 **Answer the questions**

Choose a paragraph and write some questions.

The first people in America probably arrived there about 40,000 years ago. Because of the ice, the sea level was lower then and there was dry land between Asia and North America. People crossed over the land and travelled south into North and South America.

Answer the questions.

1 When did people arrive in America?
2 Where did they come from?
3 Why was the sea level lower?

Idea 4 **True or false?**

Choose a paragraph and write some true and false sentences.

The first people in America probably arrived there about 40,000 years ago. Because of the ice, the sea level was lower then and there was dry land between Asia and North America. People crossed over the land and travelled south into North and South America.

Are these sentences true, false, or is the information not in the text?

1 The people came from South America.
2 There was a lot of ice 40,000 years ago.
3 The people came on horses.

Open exercises

These exercises are freer. You can write what *you* want to write. Use your imagination!

Ideas	Examples

Idea 5 Write a newspaper story

Choose a topic, from one of the Units or from your imagination.

Make some notes first and write your story. Ask other students and your teacher for ideas and help. (Notice that headlines in English are usually in the Present tense.)

The News, March, 1642
TASMAN LANDS IN AUSTRALIA!
Last week, Abel Tasman from Holland landed in Australia. He thought he was the first person there, but he found about 300,000 Aborigines already there!
Tasman says that Australia is enormous...

Idea 6 Write a conversation

Choose two or more characters and plan a conversation between them. Use your imagination!

The King of Spain and Magellan.
King: Magellan, I've got a job for you.
Magellan: Yes, my King. What is it?
King: Well, I want you to prove that the Moluccas Islands are in the West.
Magellan: How can I do that, my King?
King: Tomorrow, you are going to sail to the Moluccas.
Magellan: Tomorrow, my King! But...

Idea 7 Write a song

Choose a song that you know and write some new words.

My English book is in my bedroom
My English book is in my bedroom.
I think it's on the floor.
I always forget to bring it.
I hope my teacher doesn't ask any more.
Oh, English, English why do I
    forget my book, my book?
English, English oh why do I forget my book?
(To the tune of 'My bonnie lies over the ocean').

Idea 8 Prepare an interview

Think of a person and a situation. For example, a person who saw a crime, a famous pop singer, an astronaut or a visitor from another planet. Prepare some questions and some answers.

David Smith has just come back from the planet Mars.
Interviewer: Well, David, can you tell us about Mars?
David: It's horrible!
Interviewer: Why?
David: It's very, very cold and it's very dark most of the time.
Interviewer: What does it look like?
David: Well, it's...

Idea 9 Write a radio or TV news report

You can write a radio or TV news report about the information in the Unit, or you can think of some news in your school, in your town or in the world. Use your imagination!

Good evening. Here is the news. Today, the government passed a new law about schools. From tomorrow, all students have to go to school from 7am to 7pm, seven days a week. Also, every student has to do a minimum of 5 hours' homework every day. We asked students what they think about the new law. This is what they said ...

Wordlist/Index

In this list you can find the words which appear in the book and their page numbers. This is also an index of language areas and topics.

Thanks and acknowledgements

Authors' thanks

The development of this course has been a large part of our lives for well over six years. During this time, we have become indebted to literally thousands of people who have so generously shared their time, skills and experience. In particular, we appreciate the constructive advice of the numerous teachers and students who helped with our initial classroom research and with the piloting, the readers and the language teaching specialists. The final version owes much to their enthusiastic involvement.

We would like to record a special 'thank you' to Peter Donovan who shared our ideals of innovation and who has provided input and support throughout. Also to James Dingle, our editor, whose hard work, professionalism, understanding and painstaking attention to detail have helped transform our ideals into reality. The final form of Level 3 owes much to the dedication and thoroughness of Helena Gomm and Sally Searby, who handled all the detailed editorial work, for which we are extremely grateful. The pride we now take in the design of the materials is due to the skilful contribution of Anne Colwell, our design manager, to whom we owe our most sincere thanks and Marcus Askwith who oversaw the completion of this Level.

We would also like to thank the Cambridge University Press sales managers and representatives around the world for all their help and support.

Finally, from Andrew, a tribute to David, aged four, for courage and strength in a hospital bed, and Lita, Daniel and Fiona for their resilience. From Diana, love and thanks to Tom, Sam and Tara for their good humour in my presence and their stoicism in my absence. Thank you for waiting so long.

Andrew Littlejohn   *Diana Hicks*

The authors and publishers would like to thank the following individuals for their vital support throughout the project:

Professor Michael Breen, Edith Cowan University, Perth, Australia; Jeff Stranks, Cultura Inglesa, Rio de Janeiro, Brazil; Laura Izarra, OSEC, São Paulo, Brazil; Sergio de Souza Gabriel, Cultura Inglesa, São Paulo, Brazil; Françoise Motard, France; Eleni Miltsakaki, Athens, Greece; Akis Davanellos, The Davanellos School of Languages, Lamia, Greece; Paola Zambonelli, SMS Volta, Bologna, Italy; Cristina Zanoni, SMS Pepoli, Bologna, Italy; Emilia Paloni, SMS Lorenzo Milani, Caivano, Italy; Gisella Langé, Legnano, Italy; Mariella Merli, Milan, Italy; Roberta Fachinetti, SMS Mastri Caravaggini, Caravaggio, Italy; Giovanna Carella, SMS Nazarino Sauro, Novate Milanese, Italy; Dominique Bertrand, SMS Giacomo Leopardi, Rome, Italy; Jan Hague, British Council, Rome, Italy; Małgorzata Szwaj, English Unlimited, Gdańsk, Poland; Alistair MacLean, NKJO, Krosno, Poland; Janina Rybienik, Przemyśl, Poland; Hanna Kijowska, Warsaw, Poland; Ewa Kołodziejska, Warsaw, Poland; Zeynep Çağlar, Beyoğlu Anadolu Lisesi, Istanbul, Turkey; Maureen Günkut, Turkey.

The authors and publishers would like to thank the following institutions for their help in testing materials from this series and for the invaluable feedback which they provided:

Colegio Sion, Rio de Janeiro, Brazil; Open English House, Curitiba, Brazil; Ginásio Integrado Madalena Khan, Leblon, Brazil; Steps in English Curso Ltda., Niterói, Brazil; Instituto Educacional Stella Maris, Rio de Janeiro, Brazil; Cultura Inglesa, São Carlos, Brazil; Colegio Bandeirantes, São Paulo, Brazil; Kaumeya Language School, Alexandria, Egypt; Victory College, Victoria, Egypt; Collège Jean Jaures, Aire-sur-la-Lys, France; Collège Louis Le Prince-Ringuet, La Fare-les-Oliviers, France; Collège de Misedon, Port Brillet, France; The Aidonoupolou School, Athens, Greece; the following language school owners in Greece: Petros Dourtourekas, Athens; Eleni Fakalou, Athens; Angeliki & Lance Kinnick, Athens; Mark Palmer, Athens; Georgia Stamatopoulou, Athens; Anna Zerbini-Vasiliadou, Athens; Shirley Papanikolaou, Heraklion; Tony Hatzinikolaou, Kos; Antonis Trechas, Piraeus; SMS Italo Calvino, Milan, Italy; SMS G Rodari, Novate Milanese, Italy; SMS L Fibonacci, Pisa, Italy; Accademia Britannica/International House, Rome, Italy; David English House, Hiroshima, Japan; British Council, Tokyo, Japan; Senri International School, Japan; Szkoła Podstawowa w Bratkówce, Poland; Primary School, Debowiec, Poland; English Unlimited, Gdańsk, Poland; 4th Independent Primary School, Kraków, Poland; Gama Bell School of English, Kraków, Poland; Kosmopolita, Łódź, Poland; Private Language School PRIME, Łódź, Poland; Szkoła Społeczna 2001, Łódź, Poland; Szkoła Podstawowa Nr 11, Nowy Sacz, Poland; Omnibus, Poznań, Poland; Szkoła Jezyków Obcych J. Rybienik i A. Ochalskiej, Przemyśl, Poland; Szkoła Podstawowa Nr 23, Warsaw, Poland; Szkoła Podstawowa Nr 320, Warsaw, Poland; Liceum Ogólnòkształcace Wschowa, Poland; Yukselis Koleji I, Ankara, Turkey; Özel Kalamis Lisesi, Istanbul, Turkey; Özel Sener Lisesi, Istanbul, Turkey.

The authors and publishers would like to thank the following for all their help in the production of the finished materials:

Gecko Limited, Bicester, Oxon for all stages of design and production. Particular thanks to David Evans, James Arnold, Wendy Homer, Linda Beveridge & Sharon Ryan; Goodfellow & Egan, Cambridge for colour scanning and reproduction. Particular thanks to David Ward; Sandie Huskinson-Rolfe of PHOTOSEEKERS for picture research; Nigel Luckhurst for photographs; Brian Martin and students at the City of Ely Community College; Heather Richards for help with selecting artists; Janet and Peter Simmonett for freelance design work throughout the project; Martin Williamson (Prolingua Productions), Diana and Peter Thompson (Studio AVP); Rich LePage and all of the actors who contributed to the recordings.

The authors and publishers are grateful to the following illustrators and photographic sources:

Illustrators: Richard Adams: pp. 32, 45; Gerry Ball: pp. 24, 25, 75; Rowan Barnes-Murphy: p. 56; James Bartholomew: pp. 12, 17, 21, 23 b, 77, 81 b; Felicity Roma Bowers: textured backgrounds; Rob Calow: pp. 11, 41, 53, 73 t, 78, 83 c, 92; Lee Ebbrell: pp. 19, 47; Goodfellow & Egan: DTP maps; Phil Healey: pp. 16, 40, 51, 52, 64, 76; Steve Lach: pp. 9, 30 t, 35, 50, 51, 55, 74, 83 t; Sally Launder: pp. 12, 80; Robin Lawrie: p. 71; Gecko Limited: DTP illustrations and graphics; Sarah McMenemy: pp. 23 t, 73 t, & exercise icons; David Mitcheson: p. 73; Mike Nicholson: p. 36, 39 b; Alan Peacock: handwriting; John Plumb: pp. Martin Sanders: p. 26; John Storey: p. 37.

Photographic sources: Ace Photo Agency/Mugshots: pp. 34 ml, 54 tl; Allsport UK Limited/Mike Powell: p. 10 umr, Allsport/Gray Mortimore: p. 10 umc, Allsport/Gary Prior: p. 10 lowml, Allsport/Steve Powell: p. 10 br; J. Alex Langley/Aspect: p. 15; Art Directors Photo Library: p. 78 tcr, Art Directors Photo Library/Ron Bambridge: p.78 c; Aspect Picture Library: p. 78 bl; Associated Press/Michael Lipchitz: p. 26 t; Owen Beattie/University of Alberta, Canada: p. 25; *Sitting Bull Chief*, c. 1831–90, D.F. Barry, Bismarck, Dakota/Bridgeman Art Library, London: p. 87 tr, *Penn and the Indians* by Benjamin West (1738-1820) (after), Friends House, Euston/Bridgeman: p. 87 bl, *Peasant Wedding*, 1568 by Pieter Brueghel the Elder (c. 1515-69), Kunsthistorisches Museum, Vienna/Bridgeman: p. 61; Britstock/Erich Bach: pp. 29 (box 1) (box 4), 30 l, 31 tr; Brown Brothers Stock Photos, USA: p. 42 (1) & (2); The J. Allan Cash Photolibrary: pp. 14 tl, 26 br, 29 bl; Mark Colwell: p. 47 m; Sabine Pusch/Black Star/Colorific: p. 86 bl, James Balog/Black Star/Colorific. p. 86 r, John Lounois/Colorific: p. 13; Corbis-Bettmann: p. 87 mr; Ecoscene/Graham Nedes: p. 59 l; Mary Evans Picture Library: p. 23; Chris Fairclough Colour Library: pp. 23 t, 38 b; FLPA/J. Zimmermann: p. 8 t; Maggie Murray/Format: p. 34 tl, Robert Harding Picture Library/Nigel Francis: p. 33 bl, RHPL/Bildagentur Schuster/Lühr: p. 33 br, RHPL/David Hughes: p. 46 br, RHPL: pp. 54, 69 r, The Hulton Getty Collection: pp. 67 um, 69 l; Sabine Pusch/The Hutchison Library: p. 86 bm, J.G. Fuller/Hutchison: p. 14 br; Image Bank/L. Castaneda: p. 30 r, Image Bank/Peter Turner: p. 59 r; Images Colour Library: pp. 11, 18 t, Tony Page/Impact: p. 30 tr; Ladd Co./Warner Brothers (courtesy Kobal): pp. 54 ml, Universal (courtesy Kobal): p. 53 tl, 54 bl, Nigel Luckhurst: pp. 38, 39, 47 b, 57, 82 (with thanks to Ginger Kipper Films), 62, 65 r, 70; Magic Eye Inc.: pp. 6, 58, 96; Martin Meyer/Network: p. 67 lowm; Paul Vorster/Impact Photos: p.79; Peter Newark's Pictures: pp. 65 tl, 67 t, 87 br; Pictor International – London: p. 78 tl; Mathew Boysons/Panos Pictures: p. 31 tl, © Philips Consumer Electronics: p. 47 tr & tl; Pictor International: pp. Thomas Broad/Planet Earth Pictures: p. 29 bl; Popperfoto: pp. 10 tl & tr, 12 t, 19, 42 (3), 44; George Bodnar/Relay Photos: p. 43 (5), Andre Csillag/Relay: p. 43 (2), Chris Walter/Relay: p. 43 (3), Relay Photos: p. 46 tr, Rex Features Limited: pp. 31 br, 33 t, Rex/Brian Rasic: p. 43 (4), Rex Interstock Limited/Paul Brown: p. 25, Rex Features Limited/Sean Mahoney: p. 78 br Rex/Sipa: p. 42 (4); NOAA/Science Photo Library: p. 30 m; Spectrum Colour Library: p. 14 t; Sporting Pictures (UK) Limited: pp. 10 lowmc, TSI/Stephen Studd: p. 26 bl, TSI/David Woodfall: p. 29 background, TSI/Robert Estall: p. 29 tr, TSI/Colin Raw: p. 29 br, TSI/Suzanne and Nick Geary: p. 66 tl, TSI/Dennis Waugh: p. 66 bl, TSI/Owen Franken: p. 66 br, T. Matsumoto/Bernard Annebicque: p. 35, Paul Koroda/Sygma: p. 86 tl, Telegraph Colour Library/Airborne Camera: p. 78 tr, Telegraph Color Library/Contact Press Images: p53 uml, 54 tc, Topham Picturepoint: pp. 29 (box 2), 43 (1); Viewfinder Colour Photo Library: p. 34 tr, 78 tcl Viewfinder/David Williams: p. 46 l; Zefa Pictures: pp. 67 b.

t = top   m = middle   b = bottom   r = right   c = centre   l = left   u = upper   low = lower

Picture Research by Sandie Huskinson-Rolfe of PHOTOSEEKERS

Cover illustration by Felicity Roma Bowers
Cover design by Dunne & Scully.
Design and production handled by Gecko Limited, Bicester, Oxon.
Colour scanning and reproduction: Goodfellow & Egan, Cambridge.
Sound recordings by Martin Williamson, Prolingua Productions, at Studio AVP and North American Sound recordings by Rich Le Page.
Freelance editorial work by Helena Gomm.

Unit 14   Exercise 1

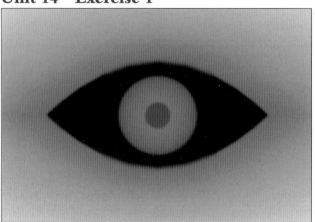